A Gracious Rain

A Devotional Commentary
on the Prayers for the
Church Year

RICHARD H. SCHMIDT

CHURCH PUBLISHING

HARRISBURG · NEW YORK

Hymn texts are quoted from *The Hymnal 1982* © 1985 by The Church Pension Fund, and *The Hymnal 1940* © 1943 by The Church Pension Fund. Used by permission.

Cover design by Jennifer Glosser
Interior Design by Z Design

Library of Congress Cataloging-in-Publication Data

Schmidt, Richard H., 1944-
  A gracious rain : a devotional commentary on the prayers for the church year / by Richard H. Schmidt.
    p. cm.
  ISBN 978-0-8192-2326-5 (pbk.)
  1. Hymns--Devotional use. 2. Church year meditations. 3. Episcopal Church–Hymns–History and criticism. I. Title.
  BV340.S36 2008
  242'.3–dc22
                                    2008016993

Church Publishing Incorporated
445 Fifth Avenue
New York, NY 10016

www.churchpublishing.org

5 4 3 2 1

DEDICATION

To the vessels of grace in my life:

My wife, Pam

My sons, Arne, Craig, and Andy

My daughters-in-law, Donna, Dana, and Alix

My grandchildren Michael, Xander, Cale, and Taylor

You sent a gracious rain, O God,

upon your inheritance;

you refreshed the land when it was weary.

—Psalm 68:9

CONTENTS

PREFACE

The prayers on which this book is based have been part of
Christian worship for centuries, some since early Christian
times. Although they are found in the 1979 Book of Common
Prayer of the Episcopal Church, they are not uniquely Anglican.
They express concerns, aspirations, and understandings of God
shared by Christians at all times and in all places. They provide a
model for private as well as corporate devotion.

Within the Christian liturgy, these prayers are called *collects*
(with the emphasis on the first syllable). A collect is a prayer
spoken at the beginning of the Eucharist. The text varies according
to the day.

The origin of the term *collect* is obscure. It may derive from the
Latin *collecta*, meaning assembly. In the Gregorian Sacramentary,
the term *oratio ad collectam* designated the first prayer said after the
congregation had assembled. The traditional collect in the Roman
Mass was short, concise, sober in tone, and general rather than
specific in scope. Collects in modern Roman missals and Anglican
prayer books retain these features. Marion Hatchett suggests the
word "may signify the summing up of the prayers of the individuals
who have been called to pray. Or it may designate the prayer said

at the collecting of the people at the start of the Mass, for the collect was inserted immediately after the salutation" (*Commentary on the American Prayer Book*, p. 164).

Some collects can be traced as far back as the sixth century, but most collects of ancient origin have been modified over time in accord with shifting theological emphases and social conditions. Other collects date from the Reformation, when Archbishop Thomas Cranmer composed several new ones, while at the same time translating the older collects from Latin. His style set a standard for English liturgical prose that has not been surpassed to this day. A number of the collects were written in the twentieth century, some appearing for the first time in the 1979 Book of Common Prayer. These newer collects, however, are based on biblical concepts or phrases and therefore contain traditional elements.

The meditations in this book have been in the making for over a decade. Some have been written and rewritten over the years during times of private prayer. I usually sat quietly while the words of a collect seeped through my mind, suggesting images, evoking memories, and raising questions. Most of the meditations arise from those images, memories, and questions, and many are therefore personal in nature. A few meditations are didactic, but most are anecdotal or fanciful. Many meditations begin with a thought suggested by the collect and follow it wherever it leads. Some contain portions of dialogues with God or Christ. Hymns and passages from classical devotional texts often came to mind as I reflected on a collect, and I have incorporated some of these into the meditations.

Although these meditations came to me during times of private devotion, a collect is intended for public worship. These are prayers by the church, for the church—for her faithfulness, enlightenment, strengthening, protection, and guidance. Some prayer concerns are therefore not addressed; the collects do not encompass all of Christian prayer. Petition and adoration are common in the collects; penitence and thanksgiving are rare. The larger world beyond the church is rarely mentioned. There are probably two reasons for this: intercessions for the world appear elsewhere in the church's liturgy; and the collect's purpose, coming at the beginning of worship, is to gather the church for faithful prayer and praise. The collect is part of a wider liturgy that contains other prayers as well.

From Advent through Pentecost, the Collects for the Church Year develop the themes of the liturgical seasons. After Pentecost, if a recurring theme can be identified, I would say it is the request for grace, the goodness and power of God poured upon his people. This gives most of the collects a confident, vibrant tone, a shift of emphasis from previous Anglican prayer books, in which many collects focused on the need for protection against peril.

Though universal in scope, these prayers are central to Anglican spirituality in particular. The Book of Common Prayer occupies a more prominent place in Anglicanism than liturgical texts occupy in most other Christian churches. Asked what distinctive teachings characterize their church, Anglicans typically say that their beliefs are simply those of the ancient and universal church. It is how Anglicans pray, rather than what they believe, that defines Anglicanism and affords Anglicanism its distinctive character. In fact, the Anglican understanding of Christian faith is best seen in the prayers Anglicans pray. The meditations in this book are one Anglican's effort to discern, by praying through the Collects of the Church Year, the kind of relationship into which God invites his people. But like most Christians, I do not pray as an Episcopalian, a Presbyterian, or a Roman Catholic—I pray as a *Christian*.

The collects begin on page 159 of the Book of Common Prayer and appear in two forms, a "traditional" version in Tudor English, and a "contemporary" version in modern English. Apart from verb forms and pronouns, the two versions are usually identical. For the sake of brevity, only the contemporary form is quoted in this book.

The typical collect is written according to a prescribed form, like a sonnet or haiku. Although a few collects depart from this form in some way, the standard form contains four parts in set order:

1. The collect begins with an address or invocation to God the Father (not the Son or the Holy Spirit), such as, "Almighty and everlasting God," "Gracious Father," or simply, "O God."

2. An attribute of God is then mentioned, stating the grounds on which the prayer is offered, such as, "the author and giver of all good things," or "your never-failing providence sets in order all things both in heaven and earth." In the contemporary version, this attribution is usually a declarative sentence, while in the traditional version it is usually a dependent clause modifying the address.

3. The third part of the collect is the petition, such as, "Mercifully grant that your Holy Spirit may in all things direct and rule our hearts." The petition sometimes contains an additional clause stating the expected result when the petition is granted.

4. The collect concludes with a Trinitarian doxology, which is virtually the same for all the collects and is omitted from the collects as printed in this book.

The collect for the Fifth Sunday in Lent illustrates the standard form: "Almighty God, you alone can bring into order the unruly wills and affections of sinners: Grant your people grace to love what you command and desire what you promise; that, among the swift and varied changes of the world, our hearts may surely there be fixed where true joys are to be found; through Jesus Christ our Lord, who lives and reigns with you and the Holy Spirit, one God, now and for ever. *Amen.*"

I am grateful to Nancy Duvall for reading an early draft of this book and suggesting changes, and to *Episcopal Life* and *The Living Church* for permission to reprint meditations that first appeared, in slightly modified form, in their pages.

Richard H. Schmidt
Cincinnati, Ohio
April 2008

Advent to Christmas

FIRST SUNDAY OF ADVENT

To Cast Away the Works of Darkness

Almighty God, give us grace to cast away the works of darkness, and put on the armor of light, now in the time of this mortal life in which your Son Jesus Christ came to visit us in great humility; that in the last day, when he shall come again in his glorious majesty to judge both the living and the dead, we may rise to the life immortal.

The year begins with a bleak, eerie prayer, uttered in the darkness.

I am lying on this cold, damp slab. I see only dim shadows, and I hear groans, sighs, and murmurings from them. I am not alone. And I feel unseen creatures scurrying about me, crawling over me: spiders, cockroaches, rats, mice, bats. Like them, I am a creature of the dungeon. All of us who moan in this darkness are creatures of the dungeon. Almighty God, help us!

The darkness terrifies us. It is no ordinary darkness. The scientists speak of a darkness that has no form or movement or will because it has no existence; it is neither good nor bad because it is nothing at all, the mere absence of light. But this is not the darkness of the scientists. This is a different kind of darkness, an energetic, aggressive malevolence seeking to envelop and consume us. In this darkness the seeds of self-will sprout and grow, their tendrils creeping across the dungeon floor, rooting themselves in the dampness of its cracks and wrapping themselves around our neck and limbs. They strangle what is left of our health. Cut off from light, we grow accustomed to the darkness; damp, stale air fills our lungs. We have stopped resisting the darkness. Perhaps it is normal, inevitable. Perhaps it is simply the way things are.

But God, I know that it need not be so. The darkness has not yet claimed every corner, and I can still dream of a different place and time. We all dream of it, for often I hear impassioned words—prayers?—amid the groans of those who languish beside me in these gray shadows. We dream of a garden where we walk with you in the light of day, of a time of contentment with you and all your creatures. The dream is distant but clear. We long for it, as for a blessing remembered from long ago, from before we had succumbed to the works of darkness.

We would cast away the works of darkness, O God, but our muscles have decayed in the dungeon and we lack the strength. And so we pray to you: "Almighty God, give us grace to cast away the works of darkness, and put on the armor of light." We are helpless; the power to cast away the works of darkness must come from outside ourselves. It must come from you, O God. We beg for your grace, the power that you give to cast away the works of darkness and put on the armor of light. That is what we pray for, O God—grace to begin again.

"I share your dream; indeed, I have dreamt it longer than you, and I have been waiting for you to call to me. No longer shall you lie limp on the dungeon floor. I have sought you out and joined you in the dungeon, encountering the darkness alongside you. The time of your deliverance has come. Now in the time of this mortal life I come to you. In humility I come, stooping to you that I may lift you in my arms. I come to take upon myself all your tawdry failures and acts of disobedience and to lead you home again. As I attack and banish the darkness, I shall escort you up and out of the dungeon. You will once again grow bold, and traveling in my entourage, you will glisten with reflected light. Arise, shine; for your light has come, and the glory of the Lord has risen upon you."

SECOND SUNDAY OF ADVENT

Your Messengers the Prophets

Merciful God, who sent your messengers the prophets to preach repentance and prepare the way for our salvation: Give us grace to heed their warnings and forsake our sins, that we may greet with joy the coming of Jesus Christ our Redeemer.

God sends his messengers today, just as he has always done, and like others before us, we do not heed their warnings. That is partly because we fail to recognize God's messengers. The ambiguities of human nature and the complexities of the choices we face make it hard to identify a prophet of the Lord. It seems one person's prophet is another person's heretic. If things were more clear, faithfulness might be easier. I sometimes think God loves ambiguity.

And yet, I can hear God saying, *"Ambiguity is your problem, not mine. My messages are clear enough to those who listen. Even if someone should rise from the dead, you would not believe because you do not want to believe. Hearing and responding to my messages is a matter of choice, not of clarity. If there is a problem, it is not with the message and it is not with your life situation. The problem is you."*

We don't want to repent. To repent is to change, and we want to remain as we are. We're comfortable. We don't want to turn around and begin moving in another direction. We would be faithful and walk with the Lord, but only if that means continuing as we are. We will follow Jesus so long as Jesus goes where we want to go.

And yet, we do want to repent. Our souls are conflicted. We feel exhausted, barren, empty—why do we still cling to this emptiness? We cling to the emptiness because it is *our* emptiness. We define and control it; it's all about us. To repent merely because we want to fill our emptiness would be a false repentance, because we would still be absorbed with ourselves. Genuine repentance focuses not on ourselves but on God alone. We hear the prophets speak of it, and we long for it but still hold back. Grant us the gift of true repentance, Lord. And if we are willing to repent with only half a heart, convert our whole heart. Do this in us, Lord, for your glory's sake, not for our own.

Who are the prophets of the Lord today? They are likely those who create discomfort for us, provoke and anger us, challenge what we think, say, and do. We are usually too busy to consider them; our ears are full of other noises. The prophets remain on the periphery of our awareness. They may be conservative or liberal, polished or rough, sacred or secular. They come from unexpected quarters and say unexpected things. Sometimes they seem irreverent, even blasphemous, rejecting what we would cling to. Their message is always the same: Repent. Change. Become a new person. Perhaps tomorrow we will listen to them.

By calling us to repent, the prophets prepare the way for our salvation. Repentance is not salvation, but it is the beginning of salvation. Salvation is Christ permeating us, drenching us, transforming us, rebirthing us. Repentance sets the table; Christ provides the feast. He is himself the feast.

And when Christ comes, how will we greet him? There are several possibilities: To greet him with fear. To greet him with scorn. To greet him with casual acceptance. To be so distracted with other things as not to greet him at all. Grant us grace, merciful God, that we may greet him with joy.

THIRD SUNDAY OF ADVENT

Stir Up Your Power

Stir up your power, O Lord, and with great might come among us; and, because we are sorely hindered by our sins, let your bountiful grace and mercy speedily help and deliver us.

What an odd way to begin a prayer! Does God's power need stirring up, like sugar that has settled to the bottom of a glass of tea, or a fire whose flames have died down? Has God's power lost its punch?

I think not. God is always at work, and his power is ever stirring in his world. But this is not always apparent to us. Our awareness of God's power comes and goes. It sometimes appears to us that God has been distracted or has gone to sleep, whereas it is actually we who have become distracted or gone to sleep. When we pray that the Lord stir up his power, we are really asking that he tap us on the shoulder or snap his fingers in our ear, that he arouse not himself, but us.

God has stirred me up many times when my soul had grown indolent. The most significant of these stirrings was when I encountered my wife, Pam. I believed in God when I met Pam, but my relationship to God, like everything else in my life, was largely intellectual. I read and analyzed theology, and called that faith. My faith was a dry, cold thing. Pam didn't approach God that way, nor did she respond when I sat her down to share my truth with her. I stiffened my back, determined to make her see things as I saw them. But the more I came to know Pam, the more I came to see that although she had read little theology, she understood more about God than I did. My heart and soul began to tremble, not only with love for Pam (though they trembled with that as well), but with a new love for God. That stirring up of God's power in my soul has proved typical: it has usually been through another human being that God has stirred me up.

Although every one of us can pray for the stirring up of God's power in our lives, this prayer focuses on the life of the church as a whole, upon the spirit that enlivens (or doesn't enliven) relationships among Christians.

As with individuals, when God's power is not manifest in the church, it's because we're not listening to, caring about, and treasuring each other. God cannot stir us up through another if we're not paying attention to the other. We dwell instead on things of little consequence. Ecclesiastical doctrines and polities, budgets, rubrics, calendars, schedules, programs, deciding whom to ordain, deciding who's in charge, who is in and who is out, who's right and who's wrong—I suppose discussing these things can be a means to serve and follow the Lord, but they often assume a value of their own, overshadowing everything else, soaking up our attention and energy. Discordant noises fill our ears, voices that demand, judge, gripe, and bark. Sometimes the voices come from within us. We grow exhausted and cynical. Our sin, the thing that "sorely hinders" us, is our preoccupation with the sounds of these voices. The business of the church matters only when we see the Lord in and through and beyond it. Where is God in all this busyness, we ask? God is there, in the middle of it, in the faces of one another. But sometimes we are too busy to look for him.

Lord, still our voices that you may stir our souls. "Let your bountiful grace and mercy speedily help and deliver us," that we may pause amid the clamor and listen to you.

"Here I am," you will say, "where I have always been, in your midst, immersed in the clutter and commotion of your life. Be still, all of you, and listen to me."

FOURTH SUNDAY OF ADVENT

Daily Visitation

Purify our conscience, Almighty God, by your daily visita-
tion, that your Son Jesus Christ, at his coming, may find in us
a mansion prepared for himself.

My rooms are vast. Most of them have sat empty for years. I have closets that are rarely opened, containing old hat boxes, coats that smell of mothballs, yellowed school papers and yearbooks, frayed Christmas ornaments, dresses that will never be worn again, dead bugs on the floor in the corner. I have spare bedrooms with lumpy, mildewed mattresses, back halls that creak when you walk through them, casement windows that let the cold air in, portraits of stern-looking ancestors hanging on my walls.

Most people see me only from the outside. They gaze upon my turrets and gabled eaves and imagine me a charming, elegant place, a sumptuous mansion. I am glad they do not see within me. My eaves leak. Cold, wet fear penetrates my walls and trickles down inside, staining and buckling my wallpaper. One hurt feeling, one bit of self-righteousness or self-pity leads to ten more just like it. Resentments breed within my walls like roaches. They crawl over my floors late at night. I try to banish them, but they come back. I am infested.

The linoleum in my kitchen is dried and cracking. It peels up from the floor. Beneath it lie grimy thoughts, fantasies, intentions, and memories. My wiring is dangerous, full of suppressed anger that could burst into flame and destroy me. It's all I can do to keep from burning up. Don't stand too close to me. Heavy film covers my windows, the grit of false loyalties and loves, blocking out the sunshine and the stars.

I've been afraid to let anyone in to see what really goes on inside me. I keep everyone on the outside, where I can appear elegant and gracious. My inside is closed, a dark, secret place known only to me. And because I never open my door, its hinges have rusted away; if I wanted to let you in now, I'm not sure I could.

Knock! Knock!

You can't come in. Go away.

Knock! Knock!

Who is it? What do you want?

"Behold, I stand at the door and knock; if anyone hears my voice and opens the door, I will come in to him and eat with him, and he with me."

No, not you! I know that voice! Anyone but you!

"I'm not leaving." Knock! Knock!

But I'm not ready for you! Go away. Come back another time.

"Now is the time." Knock! Knock!

Well, then. . . just a minute. I'm coming. There. I've loosened the dead bolt.

"That's not enough. Open the door. Invite me in."

Uh . . . all right. I've opened the door. Come in. But stand right there and don't look around.

"Why did you wait so long to invite me in? Did you think you had to fix yourself up first? That's my job. Look—I've brought my toolbox, my heavy-duty vacuum cleaner, new shingles and roofing nails, rolls of wallpaper and paste, new flooring, and mops and soap and scrubbing brushes. I've got it all, everything you need. I've always had it, only you wouldn't let me in. I'm going to clean every corner and crevice, fix you up, throw open your windows and let the fresh air in. I'll remodel you and make you a mansion fit for myself, for I have come not merely to visit—I have come to stay, to make my home in you, to live in you, to shine through you. All I needed was your invitation.

"But first I brought you a feast. We eat first, work later. I've been waiting so long, and I've missed you desperately while you've been

closed up inside. We've got to get to know each other, tell stories, and share some laughs together. While I set the table, you can begin telling me your deepest dreams and longings. Do not be afraid. This is not the end, but the beginning."

THE NATIVITY OF OUR LORD: CHRISTMAS DAY I

The Yearly Festival

O God, you make us glad by the yearly festival of the birth of your only Son Jesus Christ: Grant that we, who joyfully receive him as our Redeemer, may with sure confidence behold him when he comes to be our Judge.

I enjoy Christmas trees with their tinsel, hanging balls, and shiny lights. I love *Messiah*, *The Nutcracker*, and singing carols on Christmas Eve. I like looking into the faces of little children as they speak of Santa. Home-baked cookies, fresh citrus fruit arriving in corrugated boxes, hot wassail on a snowy night—all these I love.

How do these things pertain to the Incarnation of the Son of God? Most of them have more to do with sentimentality than with Christ, and some seem almost like frivolous intrusions into a holy season, peripheral things that threaten to become ends unto themselves. If that happens, Christmas will become no more significant than New Year's Day, surely the most artificial and meaningless of festivals. People blow horns the night before, ring bells, and consume too much food and drink—and for what reason? The date is an arbitrary one, and nothing changes from December 31 to January 1 except the calendar on the wall and the incidence of dull headaches the next morning. But even the headaches will pass, and the second day of January will find the world much as it was before.

If the Christmas festival becomes nothing more than decorative ornaments, pretty music, and rich hors d'oeuvres, it becomes another New Year's, an irrelevant blip in a series of meaningless events.

All these things, however, can point to a reality beyond themselves. They can become sacraments. What have bread and wine to do with the presence of Christ in the soul? Apparently nothing, yet everything to those who see beyond the apparent. What have plastic crèche scenes, jingle bells, bright red sweaters, and fruitcakes to do with the birth of the Son of God? Apparently nothing, and yet. . .

Everything depends on whether the birth of Christ changes anything in us. If it doesn't, then Christmas Day and New Year's Day are both merely days to sleep in late. But if it does, then Christmas becomes a real holiday, a holy day, the day when we receive at last our Redeemer and Judge.

We behold him "with sure confidence" as our Judge because we know our Judge is also our Redeemer. The One who peers into the deepest corners of our souls is also the One who restores our souls. We welcome the uncompromising judgment of Christ because of the enabling grace of Christ. The Lord of the universe not only holds our lives up to the light to evaluate them, but transforms what he sees. A world visited by such a Judge and Redeemer is never the same again.

How might such an event be commemorated in a yearly festival? By solemn acts of charity and devotion, certainly. But all outward observances will fall short of the reality of the event itself, and none is therefore to be dismissed out of hand. If sweet music, funny costumes, and boxes wrapped in ribbon seem too worldly a way to receive our Judge and Redeemer, could not the same have been said of gold, frankincense, and myrrh?

So let us deck the halls, bake the cookies, and light up the tree.

. ❧ .

THE NATIVITY OF OUR LORD: CHRISTMAS DAY II

This Holy Night

O God, you have caused this holy night to shine with the brightness of the true Light: Grant that we, who have known the mystery of that Light on earth, may also enjoy him perfectly in heaven.

"Why is this night different from all other nights?" That is the question the youngest boy in a Jewish family asks his father as the family begins its Passover meal. The father then begins to tell the story of God's stirring things up in his world to save his people. For Christians, this stirring up of things includes a personal appearance by God, a stepping into his world, an actual intrusion. It begins on this holy night.

It's often hard for me to see God's hand at work in the world about me, even in some vague, generalized sense. Sometimes events seem painful and senseless, with no plan or purpose, "just one damned thing after another," as a friend of mine used to say. But occasionally I catch a glimpse or hint of God. I'm not sure there's anything there. Perhaps it's my imagination, but at those moments I suspect, or at least hope, that some Mind or Power or Being lies out there somewhere, conveying to the world a plan or purpose I fail to discern. Even in these moments of groping faith, however, I would never expect this Mind/Power/ Being to enter the world in person, in the flesh, at a particular moment, at a particular place, to be seen, touched, and held.

It's the particularity of it all that stuns and affronts me. I want to insist that truth is universal and eternal. "The brightness of the true Light" must be the same everywhere, always discernible to the perceptive eye. I tell myself that if I read enough books and think enough deep thoughts, I'll see the light. If I don't, then either there is no light to see (a prospect that would depress me but that I could accept), or my eye is clouded (something I could possibly correct). It could not be that I am looking in the wrong place, for all places are surely alike.

No, they are not. The true Light shines from one place only, one obscure, unlikely, absurd little place. It is on this holy night, this night and no other, that the Light shines.

In one sense, of course, God is present at all times and in all places. A playwright is always present on stage in that he sets the stage, creates the characters, and prescribes their actions. In this way, God is always and everywhere present in his world. But something entirely different, something confounding, even frightening, happened on this holy night. God appeared in the world not as an unseen influence, but as God. God began to interact with the characters he was creating, became part of the plot he was writing. Would Shakespeare have walked on stage during a performance of *Macbeth*? And if he had, would he have appeared as William Shakespeare, playwright? It would have jolted the actors and transformed the rest of the play if he had. We would not have expected it of Shakespeare. Still less would we have expected it of God.

But God does not bind himself by what we expect. The true Light, it turns out, is not that vague, diffused light that any perceptive eye can see at any time, any place. It is a burst of light, like the light of a bomb. It is little wonder that those present on that holy night were afraid rather than soothed by the event. It was God crashing a party where he was neither expected nor wanted. We "have known the mystery of that Light on earth." The more we see and understand what happened on this holy night, the more we are transformed and our fear turns to joy as we anticipate with confidence that we will "enjoy him perfectly in heaven."

THE NATIVITY OF OUR LORD: CHRISTMAS DAY III

Our Nature Upon Him

Almighty God, you have given your only-begotten Son to take our nature upon him, and to be born [this day] of a pure virgin: Grant that we, who have been born again and made your children by adoption and grace, may daily be renewed by your Holy Spirit.

In taking our nature upon him, Christ stooped to join us and at the same time raised us to join him. His humbling is our exaltation. Christ has soldered and welded us to himself. It is not we who have searched and found Christ, but Christ who has searched and found us. We did not sign on with Christ; Christ signed on with us. This is what Orthodox Christians mean when they celebrate our "deification."

We therefore glory in our flesh, the flesh of God! When I run and stretch my lungs, taste hot bread or sip cold water, wrestle with my grandchildren, kiss and embrace my wife, lie down at night and rest my eyes in sleep—whenever I see, hear, taste, smell, or feel something, Christ is drawing me closer to himself, for Christ has made my flesh his own, and the more fully I enjoy my flesh, the more like him I become.

But it was not merely the pleasures and freedoms of life in the flesh that Christ took upon him, but its pains and limitations as well. This began at Bethlehem where he emerged from Mary's womb into a cold stable on a hard bed of prickly straw. Nor did Christ later sidestep the humiliations that attend our lives, but claimed them as his own. He therefore draws us close to him in *every* moment of our lives, in pain as well as in pleasure. However dark our minds, however wracked with pain our bodies, however disgraced our names, he hallows every moment.

We have been born again—not once, but countless times. We were born again when we were laid in the manger in Bethlehem, for all humanity was born again that night. We were born again at our baptism, for it was then that Christ claimed us by name. And since our baptism we have been born again, again, and again. Every time we awaken, we experience the grace of God as a new gift, unlike any given us before, and in that gift we are born again. Every moment is a rebirth, an untraveled highway, a fresh opportunity to give our lives to God and to receive God's gift of his life to us. Although we remember certain moments as turning points in our lives, these are not necessarily more important than the many moments we have forgotten. Their only distinction is that they are remembered. And perhaps the most important of our rebirths is remembered only by God himself. It does not matter. What matters is the present moment, the opportunity to be born yet again, to be drawn still closer to Christ, even as I write these words. This is surely what it means to be "daily renewed by your Holy Spirit."

We are "made your children by adoption and grace." As adopted children, we are distinguished from Christ, the "only-begotten Son." A child begotten by its parents assumes their nature and bears their stamp as no other child does. The adopted child does not share its parents' nature in this way, but the adopted child is sought out and chosen. God the Father did not have to seek out and choose his only-begotten Son, for the Son could never be other than the Father's own. But God sent his Son to us, to take our nature upon him, that we might become his own as well.

FIRST SUNDAY AFTER CHRISTMAS DAY

The New Light of Your Incarnate Word

Almighty God, you have poured upon us the new light of your incarnate Word: Grant that this light, enkindled in our hearts, may shine forth in our lives.

So shall my word be that goes forth from my mouth; it shall not return to me empty, but it shall accomplish that which I purpose, and prosper in the thing for which I sent it. (Isaiah 55:11)

For the word of God is living and active, sharper than any two-edged sword, piercing to the division of soul and spirit, of joints and marrow, and discerning the thoughts and intentions of the heart. (Hebrews 4:12)

In the Bible, the Word of God is the power of God in action. This prayer envisions the Word of God as light. We speak of light as distinct from its source; to our minds, sunlight and the sun are different things. But they are actually two aspects of a single thing. There would be no light but for the sun, and the sun would not be the sun apart from the light it sends forth. Sun and sunlight define each other. So, too, God and the Word of God define each other. God's power in action discloses who God is, and God would not be

God apart from his power in action.

The prayer speaks of three manifestations of the light. They are not strictly chronological, but there is a logic to their order.

The first manifestation of the light is in the person of Jesus of Nazareth, the incarnate Word, Word made flesh. The light of God shines preeminently in the person of Jesus. And because Jesus claims us for his own, the light has also been "poured upon us"—not dripped or trickled, but poured; we splash around in it.

Second, the light enters into us and is "enkindled in our hearts." It illumines every dark corner, brightens every shadow, exposes every secret. Nothing remains hidden from it. The light exposes the contents of our hearts—and then transforms our hearts into the likeness of Christ.

And finally, the light "shines forth in our lives." Through us, the Word of God illumines the world so that all creation glistens with the light; all things become an extension of the Word made flesh.

Music also comes to my mind as I think of the Word of God. The Word flows from God as music flows from a composer. We can speak of music apart from the composer, but without the composer, there would be no music. Composer and music define each other. When I sit at my piano and play a Chopin waltz or polonaise, Chopin himself is present with me. I hear his voice in the melody. I feel his passion. I see him seated in a French salon, longing for his native Poland. I sense the presence of his friend George Sand nearby. I weep, laugh, dance, and march as Chopin wept, laughed, danced, and marched. The music from the keyboard penetrates my soul; it *is* Frederic Chopin in my soul. So, too, does the incarnate Word of God penetrate and dwell in our souls.

THE HOLY NAME (JANUARY 1)

Jesus

Eternal Father, you gave to your incarnate Son the holy name of Jesus to be the sign of our salvation: Plant in every heart, we pray, the love of him who is the Savior of the world, our Lord Jesus Christ.

When a group of strangers needs to be introduced, I often say, "Tell us a story about your name." No one yet has failed to produce an interesting tale. Stories emerge about mispronunciations, ethnic prejudices, mistaken identities, misspellings and changed spellings, maiden names and married names, nicknames, meanings of names. My own name story dates from when I was in the third grade and went home from school to cry alone in my room because other children had made fun of my name.

Our names are important to us for several reasons. They give us something to live up to. My paternal grandmother who lived next door to me during my youth used to say, "Remember what your name is!" I knew what she meant—certain behaviors were not acceptable for someone named Schmidt. As a child, I was usually proud of my name and what it stood for, but there were times I wanted to run away and establish a name of my own, or live with no name at all. It wouldn't have worked; Schmidt will always be my name.

A name also gives us a set of relationships: parents, brothers and sisters, aunts and uncles. Sometimes we experience these people as a warm circle of enfolding arms and smiling faces, but at other times, we may dislike or misunderstand our relations. Either way, we share a name and we belong to each other. Name means family, and family is where you know you'll be taken in even when you've been bad.

Name also becomes synonymous with self. It is hard to imagine ourselves with any other name. That's probably why many brides nowadays want to retain their maiden name or incorporate it into a hyphenated surname. The reason I went home and cried when children made fun of my name was that I knew it wasn't really my name they were laughing at—it was me.

As Christians, we bear two names. The first is the name on our birth certificate or marriage license, different for each of us. The second is the name we share with baptized people of every place and time. It is the name with which we were marked at our baptism, the name of Jesus, or Christian.

The name of Jesus is as important to a Christian as his or her individual name. Like our individual names, it gives us something to live up to, and we are often proud of it. Some are willing to die for it. But as with our individual names, we occasionally want to forget Jesus' name, to run away from it. We feel that Jesus' name confines, stereotypes, burdens us. We long to call our own shots, make our own decisions. We may also be embarrassed or ashamed of what others who claim Jesus' name do in that name. But it never works. Christian will always be our name, not because we have taken it on, but because Christ has taken us on.

The name of Jesus also establishes us as a family. Like the prodigal walking up the road to his father's house, we find our Christian family waiting for us when we return, loving arms open wide—often with no questions asked. As in any family, bickering and misunderstandings occur, but we know that we belong to one another because we share the name of Jesus. His name is a family name, and family is where you know you'll be taken in, even when you've been bad.

Eventually, the name of Jesus also becomes synonymous with self. This does not happen instantly; rather, we grow into the likeness of Christ. Through the daily surrendering of our wills,

Christ comes more and more to fill and possess our souls.

The name of Jesus then becomes a crown upon our foreheads, a banner above us, a song to sing.

SECOND SUNDAY AFTER CHRISTMAS DAY

Wonderfully Restored

O God, who wonderfully created, and yet more wonderfully restored, the dignity of human nature: Grant that we may share the divine life of him who humbled himself to share our humanity, your Son Jesus Christ.

Imagine a gifted artisan who designed and created a sideboard from hardwoods and delicate inlays. Over time it was scratched, chipped, and damaged by water and stains. It came to resemble a shabby piece of junk. Years later, the same artisan took his tools in hand, dismantled the sideboard, sanded and restained its pieces, repaired the damaged surfaces, and rebuilt it. Both the original and the restoration are the work of the same craftsman, but the restoration is even more dear to him than the original, for he poured more of his heart into it, becoming not only its creator, but its savior as well.

God created human beings with a wonderful dignity. We were perfectly suited to our chief end, to serve, praise, and enjoy God. We shared this dignity with all created things, atoms and galaxies, mountains and seas, plants and animals, angels and archangels.

God created each and endowed each with its unique nature, each nature perfectly suited, in its own way, to serve, praise, and enjoy its Maker.

But when we turned away from God, we shattered our dignity. Even so, God did not abandon us. Instead, he came to us, took our marred nature upon himself, and restored us to a dignity more wonderful than the first. The difference between the original and the restoration is that in restoring our dignity, God took up residence within us, transforming us from his artifact into his home. God re-created us and, wrapping himself in our humanity, made his home among us.

Is our part in this entirely passive? Are we solely the recipients of grace, acted upon while not acting ourselves? In my own experiences of salvation, it is clear to me that I did not save myself. I believe this is true for everyone. And yet, surely we must consent to God's action in our lives. A drowning man can always choose to drown, even as the rescuer approaches. We are at liberty to choose to remain damaged and shabby. Our role is to grant or withhold consent. Yet even this consent is somehow an act of grace, God's gift to us:

> Lord, I did not freely choose
> you till by grace you set me free;
> for my heart would still refuse you
> had your love not chosen me.
> (Hymnal 1982, #706)

Some of the stains and disfiguring remain in us. God's work in us is not yet complete; God continues to restore and refine his creation. We indicate our willingness to be recreated by surrendering ourselves to God's will. The words of Charles Wesley express our prayer:

Finish then thy new creation;
Pure and spotless let us be;
let us see thy great salvation
perfectly restored in thee:
changed from glory into glory,
till in heaven we take our place,
till we cast our crowns before thee,
lost in wonder, love, and praise.
(*Hymnal 1982*, #657)

Epiphany Season

THE EPIPHANY (JANUARY 6)

Face to Face

O God, by the leading of a star you manifested your only Son to the peoples of the earth: Lead us, who know you now by faith, to your presence, where we may see your glory face to face.

The author of the Epistle to the Hebrews has given us a famous definition of faith, as "the assurance of things hoped for, the conviction of things not seen" (Hebrews 11:1). I've never liked this definition because it seems so tentative, so ambiguous. I want more than to hope for something: I want to know. When I look about a room and note the location of the furniture, I'm sure of what I see. But when I turn my eyes inward or upward (I am not even sure where to turn them) to search for the meaning of my existence, the fog seems to descend and I am sure of little.

We know God now by faith, and faith is always a risk, never a certainty. That means our understanding of God is at best partial and tentative. Sometimes we feel close to God and are confident of our faith. At other times, it is as if we catch but a glimpse of something—God?—out of the corner of our eye, but when we turn to look directly at this something, it has moved elsewhere. Did we really see anything? We think so, though we can't be sure, and if we could be sure we saw something, could we be sure it was God?

I suspect many people long for the certainty that is never quite granted us in this life. That would account for the popularity of tidy little religions that claim to answer every question. The trouble is that in eliminating the mystery, such religions trivialize

God and remove the very thing that inspires worship. It's like Dorothy and her companions on the road to Oz. The wizard of Oz inspired awe only so long as he remained veiled.

The wizard of Oz was also a fake, of course. After Dorothy and her party penetrated the curtain, they found the wizard to be nothing more than an insecure little man, a reflection of themselves. We sometimes wonder: if we could look at God, would we discover that God is a fake?

Maybe. But maybe not. We cannot be sure while we journey through the land of Oz. Not being sure is part of faith; we do not need faith when we can be sure. Knowledge of a sort comes with faith, but certainty does not.

Moreover, the road we travel sometimes feels less like colorful, charming Oz than like John Bunyan's "wilderness of this world." We are grateful for the happy times of confidence and affirmation, but at other times we slog through the Slough of Despond, tarry in Doubting Castle, are lured by the wares of Vanity Fair, and tremble in the Valley of the Shadow of Death. The wilderness lays bare our ignorance and helplessness. But this is the only road to the Celestial City. If we would see the glory of the Lord face to face, there is no other way.

Perhaps the most awful thing about the wilderness is that God is not the only presence there: the devil also makes his home in the wilderness. He taunts us as we travel through, feeding our doubts, mocking our confidence, and seeking to lure us aside from our journey. We battle such temptations as someone walking through a stiff wind battles the swirling air.

So it was with Moses also. Moses spent years in exile, confronted Pharaoh, passed through the Red Sea, stood before the fire and smoke, wandered in the wilderness, and battled a rebellious people, all before the Lord spoke to him face to face, as friend to friend (Exodus 33:11). First the wilderness, then, at the end of the wilderness, intimacy with the Lord.

Could it be that it is only possible to gaze upon the glory of God face to face, to converse with God as with an intimate friend, after we have confronted the devil, faced him down, and followed the star into the darkness?

· ☙ ·

FIRST SUNDAY AFTER THE EPIPHANY: THE BAPTISM OF OUR LORD

Baptized into His Name

Father in heaven, who at the baptism of Jesus in the River Jordan proclaimed him your beloved Son and anointed him with the Holy Spirit: Grant that all who are baptized into his Name may keep the covenant they have made, and boldly confess him as Lord and Savior.

"You are my beloved Son; with you I am well pleased." Those were the words spoken to Jesus by a voice from heaven at his baptism (Mark 1:11). For many years, I found this story discomforting. When I listened to other Bible stories, I often imagined myself in the scene, even one of the characters in the story. But when the account of Jesus' baptism was read, it was as if I were standing on the fringe of the crowd, far removed from the events. I felt heavy and lonely when I heard the story.

One day I realized why. It was because of those words spoken by the voice from heaven. The words were right, but they were spoken to the wrong person—*those were the words I wanted spoken to me!*

Years later, I realized that the voice from heaven wasn't speaking only to Jesus. Millions upon millions of unworthy souls splashed in the Jordan with Jesus that day, and I was one of them. When he plunged into the water, Jesus took me in his arms and dunked me with him. That was my baptism, too. Together with Christians through the ages, I have been baptized into the death of

Jesus Christ, and with them, I live in the power of his resurrection. My sins have been forgiven and I have been raised to the new life of grace. Because I was a companion of Jesus in the Jordan that day, I too am a beloved son, and my heavenly Father is well pleased with me. The voice was speaking to me.

This new relationship with God is called a "covenant." A covenant is an agreement between two parties. Our part of the agreement is to promise, with God's help, to live a Christian life. But the covenant was initiated by God. As God's part of the covenant, he promises to accept us in something like the way human parents accept their children. As a father, I love my children not because they are good, which they sometimes are and sometimes are not, but because they are mine. Our baptism is God's signature on our adoption papers that we are his.

People sometimes ask whether only the baptized are God's beloved children. They say it seems arbitrary, perhaps even cruel of God, to love only those who happen to have been baptized. What of those who die unbaptized? It is a silly question, based on an understanding of baptism as a magic trick, a human action that, like voodoo, is thought to change God's disposition toward a person. Baptism is the seal of God's love, the public announcement of it, but it does not create God's love, any more than a handshake creates an agreement between two partners. God loves us from the moment he conceives us in his mind. It is God's nature to love, limitlessly, with or without our liturgical ceremonies, and we can trust God to do what it is his nature to do.

My own baptism became increasingly important to me as this understanding grew in my mind. I wanted to know when God had publicly announced that Richard Hanna Schmidt was his beloved son. I knew I had been baptized as a young child, both because my parents assured me of it and because I dimly remembered the occasion: my younger brother and I were baptized on the same day, and I recall being disciplined for misbehaving during the ceremony. But how old was I? When did that event occur? My parents retained no record of my baptism. I wrote to the pastor of the First Presbyterian Church of Shelbyville, Kentucky, where the baptism had taken place. He wrote back that the records of the church from the 1940s were in disarray in the bottom of a flooded bank vault and that it might be impossible to learn the date of my baptism. I was disappointed to receive his letter, but I had lived happily for forty years without knowing the date, so I figured I could continue to do so. I put it out of my mind.

But the pastor did not forget my inquiry. Three years later, I received another letter from him: "I was in the bank vault this week sorting through the damaged church records, and I came across the record of your baptism. You were baptized on April 4, 1948." I remember trembling as I gazed at the paper on which the date was written. I looked it up immediately. April 4 was the Sunday after Easter that year. In the Episcopal Church, this is the Sunday when we read about Thomas, the outsider, who was not with the others when Jesus appeared to them that first Easter night and who couldn't bring himself to believe the implausible tale they told him when he returned. How very fitting, I thought. I've always identified with Thomas. I am delighted to have been baptized on the day the church recalls the event for which Thomas is chiefly remembered. The Second Sunday of Easter has now become my own personal holy day. Each year, I say special prayers that day, in private, to thank God for receiving me into his loving arms.

Second Sunday After the Epiphany

The Light of the World

Almighty God, whose Son our Savior Jesus Christ is the light of the world: Grant that your people, illumined by your Word and Sacraments, may shine with the radiance of Christ's glory, that he may be known, worshiped, and obeyed to the ends of the earth.

The true light that enlightens every man was coming into the world. (John 1:9)

Again Jesus spoke to them, saying, "I am the light of the world; he who follows me will not walk in darkness, but will have the light of life." (John 8:12)

Once during my student days, I had occasion to spend the night with a classmate who lived in the basement of an old rooming house. I had never visited his room and knew nothing about the house apart from its location. My friend and I were attending different meetings that night, and he gave me a key to the house in case I arrived before he did.

It was nearly 10:00 p.m. when I arrived, and no one was there. I found the basement door but had trouble unlocking it because the parking area was not lit and the entryway was dark. I felt around the door until I located the lock, placed my key in the lock,

and turned it. The door opened. I entered the basement and felt on
the wall for a light switch. There was no light switch. The hall—if
I was standing in a hall—was totally dark. I stepped hesitantly into
the darkness, moving my hands in the air before me to avoid
bumping into something. I located a wall and began to feel my way
along it. My friend had said his room was the second room on the
left. I found what I guessed was the door to his room, opened it,
and entered the room.

Still I could see nothing. I felt again for a light switch on the
wall but failed to find one. I had begun to feel vaguely frightened,
as if I were in the midst of a forest with dangerous animals lurking
nearby. I bumped into a chair, then a desk—surely there would be
a lamp on the desk. Yes! My hand touched a lamp. I found the
switch and turned it, and the light came on.

I stood there for a moment and looked around me. There were
my friend's jacket and his books—this was indeed his room. The
room contained an easy chair, a couch, and a bed, all familiar,
ordinary objects, hardly things to be afraid of. I felt silly at having
been frightened. The light in the bedroom shone into the hall. Still
standing in the doorway, I turned and looked into the hall. I could
see a small table and an umbrella stand, and the door I had entered
from the outside. And there on the wall was a light switch, which
I had somehow missed. I walked over to it and turned it on.
A ceiling light suddenly illumined the entire hall. The light
transformed a murky, ominous environment into an orderly,
benign environment.

That experience helped me understand what Jesus might have
meant when he said he was the light of the world (John 8:12; 9:5).
The world had been a dark place, filled with baffling mysteries.
People had stumbled around in the dark trying to make sense of it
all and figure out what to believe and what to do. Some people had
seen flickers of light and had managed to get closer to the truth
than others, but darkness was pervasive.

It is as if Christ is the floodlight illuminating everything.
Dangers are not removed, but they are now seen as part of a larger
picture, full of grace and truth. This includes the dangers that lurk

within us—bitterness, resentment, self-will. These perils to the soul linger for a time, but when they are exposed to the light, they begin to loosen their hold over us, as mud is dried by the sun. Illumined by Christ's word and sacraments, we too begin to shine with the radiance of his glory, looking forward to the promised day when Christ will be known, worshiped, and obeyed to the ends of the earth.

During the rest of the year, we in the church look within us and about us. We examine the various things that the light reveals and ponder the implications. Some of the things the light discloses reassure us; others challenge and convict us. The rest of the year is for examining and pondering what the light reveals. Epiphany is the time to celebrate the fact that at last the darkness has ended and the light arrived.

THIRD SUNDAY AFTER THE EPIPHANY

The Glory of His Marvelous Works

Give us grace, O Lord, to answer readily the call of our Savior Jesus Christ and proclaim to all people the Good News of his salvation, that we and the whole world may perceive the glory of his marvelous works.

Church work has but one purpose: that we and the whole world may perceive the glory of the marvelous works of Jesus Christ. I realize that is the purpose of church work when I stop to think about it, but I rarely stop to think about it. I am usually so preoccupied with the work itself that I give little thought to why I do it.

In my years as a parish priest, I often exhausted myself with church work and then stayed awake nights thinking about church work. How would we motivate volunteers and keep them from burning out? How would we minister to youth, parents, shut-ins, newcomers, old-timers? How would we raise more money, or learn to manage with less? Who would repair the furnace, mow the grass, set up the chairs? How would we pacify the malcontents, stir the listless, comfort the grieving, embrace the lonely, instruct the searching, discipline the wayward, and generally hold the whole blessed mess together?

Underlying these questions that so often consumed me was a deeper question that I rarely asked: why did I bother with any of this? I could have made a living in other ways. What motivated me to spend such time and energy on these things? My motivations were varied. Sometimes I wanted to look good, and I knew I would look good if my congregation flourished. I worked hard to look good. Sometimes I felt I had to prove I was a worthy person. To whom did I want to prove it? My parents? My peers? My bishop? Myself? God? I'm not sure to whom I wanted to prove it, but I sometimes felt compelled to prove it to someone. At other times my motivation was to protect things I love: the church's liturgy and music, her solemn buildings, the network of friendships I found among her people. I worked to hold onto things precious to me. And sometimes I glimpsed a vision of people working together to make a better world and sought to help them make that vision a reality. I worked to make a better world.

I now know that none of this will matter in the end. Any reputation I acquire, anything I prove about myself, everything dear to me, and anything I might achieve in the world—all these will pass. They are like sand castles that look substantial when the tide is out but vanish without a trace when the tide returns a few hours later. There is pleasure in building sand castles, as there often is in church work, and if we seek pleasure, church work may be a harmless place to find it. But the kinds of pleasures found in the church are also found elsewhere, and if that's all we seek, we can perhaps find it with less cumbersome baggage in other places.

Church work is worth the effort only if our reason for doing it is that the world may perceive the glory of the marvelous works of Jesus Christ.

Glory is the reason for church work, and no other work is done for the sake of glory. The church directs our attention to the glory of Christ, that shimmering quality that we occasionally glimpse, indicating Christ's presence in the seemingly dull world around us. When we discover Christ incarnate in his creation, drab becomes bright, grimy becomes sparkling, cold becomes warm, pale becomes colorful, dissonance becomes harmony. We see beyond the veil to the numberless places where heaven touches earth. These are moments of glory; they are "his marvelous works."

Throughout our lives, we discover his glory all along the way. This we cannot do if we are preoccupied with church work. We must preoccupy ourselves with glory. "The Good News of his salvation" is that if we have eyes to see, we can glimpse glory everywhere, for he has drenched the world with his glory, like the dew of the morning.

FOURTH SUNDAY AFTER THE EPIPHANY

You Govern All Things

Almighty and everlasting God, you govern all things both in heaven and on earth: Mercifully hear the supplications of your people, and in our time grant us your peace.

It seems odd that on this Sunday we acknowledge at the beginning of the Eucharist that God governs all things both in heaven
and on earth, only to pray a few moments later, in the Lord's
Prayer, that his will be done on earth as in heaven. If God rules
both in heaven and on earth, why is his will done only in heaven?

It has to do with human freedom. God does not compel us to
obey him, and if we choose to turn our backs on him, he allows it.
It is as if God says to us, *"My will is that your will be done on earth."*

God wants us to obey him because we love him. Love is
not love unless it is freely chosen, for freedom must include the
possibility of rejection. Otherwise, we would be human robots or
computers, like the women in the movie *The Stepford Wives*. God
could have programmed us to do whatever he commanded, to
behave "lovingly," but that would not really be love. He chose
instead to endow us with the freedom to decide for ourselves
whether to love and obey him. A deeper relationship is possible
where there is freedom: it's hard to love a robot, and robots cannot
love in return. The risk is that free creatures will abuse their
freedom, inflicting pain upon one another and grieving the heart
of God. It's a risk God was willing—and is still willing—to take.

This freedom has brought mixed results. There are instances
of obedience on the part of human beings, behavior rightly called
divine. Everyone has seen the fruit of the Spirit—love, joy, peace,
patience, kindness, goodness, faithfulness, gentleness, self-
control—manifested in some remarkable, soaring way: A mother
goes hungry to provide for her children. A homeless man beneath
a bridge shares his blanket with another. A teacher remains after
school to work with a student who needs special help. A prosper-
ous nation forgoes some domestic amenity to aid a struggling
nation elsewhere in the world. One friend forgives another for a
broken confidence. A soldier sacrifices his life for his buddy. A
recovering alcoholic gets up in the middle of the night to help
another alcoholic. A people victorious in war deal generously with
the losers.

But these moments of grace are balanced—outweighed, it often
seems—by instances of cruelty, prejudice, selfishness, gluttony, and

vainglory, both in individual relationships and in social structures. God's decision to grant us freedom carries an immense cost.

This prayer does not specify what "the supplications of your people" are, asking only that in hearing them, God will grant us his peace. Perhaps our supplication should be that God intensify his wooing of us, whisper—or shout—his words of love into our ears until we hear, court us until we willingly succumb, batter the doors of our hearts until we fling them open and welcome our Lord into his rightful home.

Then we will enjoy his peace, not an imposed peace, like the "peace" of an occupied nation or of a man kept in line by external constraints, and not a tense peace, like the "peace" between two people who distrust each other but refrain from outward hostility, but a serene well-being, a harmony of wills, freely chosen, between God and his people. Trust and mutuality will ennoble relationships among nations, and the conflicts within each fractured soul will give way to serenity and contentment. In that day, it will no longer be necessary to pray "Thy will be done," for the will of God will be an accomplished fact, on earth as in heaven.

FIFTH SUNDAY AFTER THE EPIPHANY

That Abundant Life

Set us free, O God, from the bondage of our sins, and give us the liberty of that abundant life which you have made known to us in your Son our Savior Jesus Christ.

The pelican flaps his wings and then glides motionless, inches above the surface of the bay. Then he flaps his wings and glides some more. When he is ready, he rises a few feet into the air until he spots a fish near the surface of the water. Then he plops into the bay for his breakfast. Tired at last, he finds a piling beyond the pier where he takes a nap. Or is he watching me as he sits like a statue on his piling in the bay?

I am sure the pelican is content with his pelicanhood. He flaps, glides, rises, plops, eats, and naps. Then he does it all over again. He is not angry or grieved or anxious because he cannot climb an oak tree or burrow into the ground. The pelican is free because he does as a pelican is meant to do and is content to do it.

We are not free like the pelican. God created us to serve and enjoy him—as human beings. But we are not content to be who we are. At times we want to be an animal or a bird—perhaps the pelican, in fact. If only we could flap and glide and rise as the pelican does, we'd be happy, we tell ourselves. At other times we want to be some other person, a wealthier, more famous, more handsome, or more influential person. We tell ourselves we'd be happy if only we could be what that other man is and do as he does. At other times, we want to be an angel or spirit, one who gazes upon the face of God and who is not troubled by insoluble mysteries. We tell ourselves we'd be happy if only we could see what we cannot see and know what we cannot know.

The chains that bind us from claiming the abundant life that God has made known in Jesus are inside our souls and are self-imposed. Because we will not accept who we are, will not serve and enjoy our Maker as the person he has created us to be, we choose captivity over freedom. Set us free, O God, for although we have put ourselves into these chains, we cannot by our own devices break them. The habits of discontent are so ingrained in us that only a power beyond our own can eradicate them.

I remember two tales, related by Martin Buber in his *Tales of the Hasidim*: Rabbi Simha Bunam of Pzhysha once said, when he had grown old and blind, "I should not like to change places with our father Abraham! What good would it do God if Abraham became like blind Bunam, and blind Bunam became like Abraham? Rather than have this happen, I think I shall try to grow a little over and beyond myself." The same idea was expressed by Rabbi Zusya of Hanipol, when he said, "In the world to come I shall not be asked: 'Why were you not Moses?' I shall be asked: 'Why were you not Zusya?'"

SIXTH SUNDAY AFTER THE EPIPHANY

Nothing Good without You

O God, the strength of all who put their trust in you: Mercifully accept our prayers; and because in our weakness we can do nothing good without you, give us the help of your grace, that in keeping your commandments we may please you both in will and deed.

As a young man, I intended to do it all, and to do it all very well. In my work as a priest, I would preach, teach, counsel the troubled, visit the sick, comfort the afflicted, and administer the day-to-day operations of my parish. I would excel at all these things. At the same time I would be a loving and faithful husband, father, and friend. Everything about my personal life, my career, and my relationship to God would be in perfect order. I would see to it myself.

I thought in those days that I trusted God. Thinking and talking about God consumed much of my time, and I believe those thoughts and words often approached the truth. But underlying it all was the assumption that everything depended on what I did.

God wasn't going to save me because I didn't need saving. I was going to do the saving—of myself, of the church, of the world, perhaps even of God. I believed I trusted God; I wanted to trust God, was trying to trust God—but I didn't know that before I could trust God, I had to abandon my own strength and relinquish the skill and competence I had worked so hard to acquire.

I began to understand this when I realized that although I could accomplish many things through the force of my personality, intellect, diligence, and ability, none of these things would matter. Those accomplishments were like the house built on the sand that, when the rain fell and the floods came and the winds blew against it, fell with a great crash. The people around me who loved me knew that my house was falling before I knew it. When I finally knew it myself, it was as if the first gray hint of dawn had become visible above the dark horizon.

I began to see myself no longer as the super-competent Christian leader, but as a kind of joke. I was a balloon that bounced proudly around the room when it was full of air but went nowhere. Then someone (God?) punctured it. Much to its surprise, as it lay on the floor, limp, empty, perforated, and defeated, the wind picked it up and carried it through an open window into the sky.

St. Paul learned a similar lesson. I envision him being full of himself during his early ministry. He did not hesitate in his early letters to give advice, some of it solicited and some of it, I suspect, unsolicited. It was good advice, of course. But in his later epistles, Paul shows a happy acceptance of himself and of others and a self-effacing humor not found in his earlier letters.

I think of Paul as smiling, perhaps even giggling, when he wrote, "To keep me from being too elated by the abundance of revelations, a thorn was given to me in the flesh, a messenger of Satan, to harass me, to keep me from being too elated. Three times I besought the Lord about this, that it should leave me; but he said to me, 'My grace is sufficient for you, for my power is made perfect in weakness'" (2 Corinthians 12:7–9). I can envision the puffed up, proud, diligent Paul, "too elated by the abundance of revelations." He needed that thorn in the flesh.

Paul was, I believe, speaking of his reputation and competence when he wrote (and again, I envision him smiling), "I count everything as loss because of the surpassing worth of knowing Christ Jesus my Lord. For his sake I have suffered the loss of all things, and count them as refuse"—garbage, waste, trash, things not evil in themselves, but not worth holding onto (Philippians 3:8).

And so we come to "the help of your grace," Lord. Give it to us, we ask, because without it, nothing matters. With it, we can keep your commandments both in will and deed because we won't really be the ones keeping them: you will keep your commandments for us, within us, among us, and in spite of us.

Seventh Sunday after the Epiphany

Your Greatest Gift

O Lord, you have taught us that without love whatever we do is worth nothing: Send your Holy Spirit and pour into our hearts your greatest gift, which is love, the true bond of peace and of all virtue, without which whoever lives is accounted dead before you. Grant this for the sake of your only Son Jesus Christ.

Many people feel that the elder brother in the parable of the prodigal son (Luke 15:11–32) got a raw deal. "Why is he made out to be the bad guy?" people say. "He obeyed all the rules, worked hard, maintained the family estate, was there when his father needed him. The younger brother disrupted the family by running away from home, wasted the family's savings, and failed even to stay in touch. The elder brother had a right to be angry. If either brother deserved to have a party thrown for him, it was the elder brother!"

Those who sympathize with the elder brother are right about one thing: he had behaved himself, and the younger brother had not. But this story is not about correct behavior. It is about love. The elder brother's behavior was meticulously proper, but his heart was encased in ice. He was good because he expected to be rewarded, as a laborer works for his wages. His world had no room for forgiveness, reconciliation, grace, or a second chance. If he hugged anyone, it was when protocol required it, never as an act of spontaneous joy.

Good behavior comes easily to people who believe it will be recognized and rewarded. Love does not come easily; it is a gift.

The love of which the Bible speaks rests upon grace, not rewards. It is usually thought of as a giving of oneself with no thought of receiving anything in return, for no reason other than the pleasure and well-being of the beloved. We see this love in the father who threw a party for a son who not only possessed nothing to give in return, but who deserved nothing. The father's only thought was to receive his son home again and make him happy after years of privation. The father is, of course, a type for God, and the father's love in the story suggests the quality of love that flows from the heart of God.

There is, however, another aspect of love that is less often recognized: the love expressed in receiving a gift one does not deserve. It may be more blessed to give than to receive, but it is also easier to give than to receive. The giver is in control. Have you ever noticed how much more enjoyable it is to watch as someone opens a gift from you than to open a gift from someone else? Everyone enjoys being in a position to dispense favors; it is hard to enjoy receiving charity. To accept a gift gracefully is to acknowledge one's need, dependence, indebtedness, even one's unworthiness. It calls for a surrender of the ego. To receive a gift is to give a gift in return, the gift of power. Receiving can be (though like giving, it is not always) an act of devotion and commitment, an act of love. In receiving as much as in giving, rewards do not enter in.

I often see this when I visit in homes and hospitals where someone is critically ill. I can tell when the relationships in the room are loving. The caregiver and the one cared for accept one another's roles, even when anxiety is high. One person loves by caring; the other loves by graciously accepting the care offered. In such a relationship, both giving and receiving are natural, unselfconscious expressions of a shared love that has known thousands of such expressions before.

What we do matters less than the spirit in which we do it. The elder brother did the right things but with the wrong spirit. Though he lived, he was accounted dead. The younger brother did the wrong things until he surrendered his will and slouched back home expecting to beg for favors. When the father embraced him, he accepted the embrace; when the father put shoes on his feet, he got up and danced; when the father killed the fatted calf, he ate and made merry. Though he was dead, yet he lived.

EIGHTH SUNDAY AFTER THE EPIPHANY

The Father's Will

Most loving Father, whose will it is for us to give thanks for all things, to fear nothing but the loss of you, and to cast all our care on you who care for us: Preserve us from faithless fears and worldly anxieties, that no clouds of this mortal life may hide from us the light of that love which is immortal, and which you have manifested to us in your Son Jesus Christ our Lord.

R on DelBene has said that most Christians have five thoughts in the back of their minds about the will of God. They are that (1) there is one will of God for my life; (2) it is eternal; (3) God knows what it is; (4) I don't; and (5) my job is to find out what it is and do it.

I'd always thought of God's will pretty much like that. When faced with a decision, I'd pray to God to reveal his will for me, show me what I was supposed to do. When the decision was an important one, this praying was intense. The topic was often job-related, whether to seek new work, or to accept or decline a new position when it was offered. I recall once saying, "You know how confounded I am, Lord. Just give me a clear sign, and I promise to do your will—but please, just give me a sign!" Almost always, no sign was given (or if it was, I failed to recognize it). I remained as perplexed after praying as I was before. It seemed God wanted me to tough it out without the longed for sign.

I eventually came to see that I was defining the will of God the wrong way. I had made the will of God an external thing, separate from God, from myself, and from my relationship to God. The will of God became like the command of a parent to a child to "eat your vegetables." The reason it is good to eat vegetables has nothing to do with the relationship of parent and child. A child could learn about nutrition in school and decide on his own to eat his vegetables, without any relationship to a parent at all.

The will of God cannot be separated from God and can be known only as part of a relationship to God. The will of God for us *is* a relationship. One might obey all God's commandments for reasons having nothing to do with God—out of spiritual pride, say, or to gain the respect of one's peers. We see examples of this in the elder brother (Luke 15:25–32) and the rich man (Mark 10:17–22). God's will for us is like a parent's will for a child. Parents want their children to behave properly, but a parent takes no pleasure in a child who merely behaves properly. What parents long for is that children return the parents' love for them, a love often indicated by respectful behavior. God longs for us to return his love—that is the will of God.

The clauses that compose the attribution to this collect all describe features of the loving relationship that our heavenly Father desires with us.

It is possible "to give thanks for all things" only when we experience the love of God undergirding all things. This is not difficult during happy times, but when deprivation or tragedy come upon us, it is easy to lose sight of God's love for us. Then, more than at any other time, we must remember Jesus, who was no stranger to deprivation and tragedy and in whom we are assured that nothing can separate us from the love of God (Romans 8:31–39).

To "fear nothing but the loss of you" requires that we see all other things—human relationships, possessions, our lives—as part of our loving relationship to God. This does not mean that we cease to care about these things in themselves, but that we understand that when we lose them (as we will someday), the love of God will remain to see us through.

We "cast all our care on you who care for us" because we know that we depend on God every moment of our lives—like the birds of the air and the lilies of the field (Matthew 6:25–34), and like the child held in her mother's arms.

To ask God to "preserve us from faithless fears and worldly anxieties" is to ask him to perfect our love: "There is no fear in love, but perfect love casts out fear" (1 John 4:18). "If our love were but more faithful, we should take him at his word; and our life would be thanksgiving for the goodness of the Lord" (*Hymnal 1982*, #469). "Faithless fears and worldly anxieties" easily overwhelm us when we lose our vision of that other world where God reigns and his will is done, and the way to keep our vision focused there is to look into the eyes of Jesus, the Word made flesh, the Prince of heaven come to earth.

. ✑ .

LAST SUNDAY AFTER THE EPIPHANY

The Holy Mountain

O God, who before the passion of your only-begotten Son revealed his glory upon the holy mountain: Grant to us that we, beholding by faith the light of his countenance, may be strengthened to bear our cross, and be changed into his likeness from glory to glory.

This Sunday and its collect mark the transition from Epiphany to Lent. The Epiphany lessons and prayers point to the growing illumination around us. In the gospel passages appointed for the season, the glory of Christ is manifest in one place after another: his baptism in the Jordan River, conversing with Nathaniel in Bethsaida, the marriage feast at Cana, the synagogue in Nazareth, casting out the unclean spirit at Capernaum, on the lake with the miraculous catch of fish, and finally, on this Last Sunday after the Epiphany, on the Mount of the Transfiguration. In Lent, we shall begin a steady movement toward the ultimate manifestation of Christ's glory, his passion and resurrection.

The story of the transfiguration (Matthew 17:1–8; Mark 9:2–8; Luke 9:28–36) and this prayer serve both as a culmination of the Epiphany themes and as a hint of that still greater glory to be manifest in Jerusalem on Good Friday and Easter Day.

From the vantage point of Epiphany, the transfiguration is the paramount story of glory. Three of Jesus' disciples gaze upon their Lord, astonishingly transfigured, blazing like the sun and flanked by Moses and Elijah, legendary figures whom the disciples could not have recognized by any normal means.

Peter, showing his humanity here as elsewhere, suggests that three booths be constructed, enabling the three holy men—and the three disciples, no doubt—to remain indefinitely in the glow of the mountaintop. But the mountaintop is only a temporary stop on a journey that must lead to Jerusalem, and the vision granted to the disciples there is to strengthen them for what is to come. In asking to remain on the mountaintop, Peter is like most of us. When granted a "mountaintop experience," we usually seek to preserve and perpetuate it, to pickle it, so to speak. But God grants us such experiences—rarely, for most of us—in order to strengthen us for what is to come in the sometimes terrifying valley below:

> Not always on the mount may we
> Rapt in the heav'nly vision be:
> The shores of thought and feeling know,
> The Spirit's tidal ebb and flow.
>
> The mount for vision: but below
> The paths of daily duty go,
> And nobler life therein shall own
> The pattern on the mountain shown.
> (*Hymnal 1940*, #571)

Our life and destiny are in seamy, violent Jerusalem, not on the Mount of the Transfiguration. Invariably, this will entail the bearing of a cross. Christian life is impossible without bearing a cross, not because God wants us to suffer, but because God wants us to live and living comes only as the result of dying. I suspect that is why Luke informs us that the transfigured Jesus was talking with Moses and Elijah "of his departure, which he was to accomplish at Jerusalem." In Jerusalem, Christ will suffer and be glorified; it is precisely in his suffering that his glory is most brilliantly manifest.

Lent

ASH WEDNESDAY

You Hate Nothing You Have Made

Almighty and everlasting God, you hate nothing you have made and forgive the sins of all who are penitent: Create and make in us new and contrite hearts, that we, worthily lamenting our sins and acknowledging our wretchedness, may obtain of you, the God of all mercy, perfect remission and forgiveness.

The opening affirmation of this prayer sets the tone for a holy Lent: God hates nothing he has made. This affirmation comes as a surprise to some people. A woman came into my office some years ago, walking hesitantly, hunched over, ashen in the face. At first I thought she had suffered some calamity. But as she began to talk, I realized that the outward circumstances of her life were pleasant enough—her pain came from within. "I just can't believe that God could actually love me," she said. I asked whether she had done something terrible. "Nothing," she said. "I just feel so rotten and dirty and unworthy inside. God couldn't possibly love me." As we talked, she told me the story of her life, including an abusive upbringing full of censure and condemnation, with frightening warnings of the wrath of God.

I opened the prayer book to the Collect for Ash Wednesday and read it to her. "That says God hates nothing he has made, which includes you," I said. "Do you believe this?" She mumbled that she did not. I then asked her to visualize herself in heaven, standing before Jesus, while singing the words of the well-known hymn: "Just as I am: thou wilt receive; wilt welcome, pardon, cleanse, relieve." I asked her whether she believed those words. She said she couldn't believe them. I then asked her to visualize Jesus holding a ledger book in his hand with her name on the cover. The ledger book contained a list of all her offenses, small and large. Jesus speaks to her:

> *Goodness, goodness me! I've had to add so many pages to your ledger book to list all your offenses that I can hardly lift the book onto the table to add up the columns! You've got enough sheets in your ledger book to open up a library! But no matter. I only kept your ledger book so that I could have the fun of watching your face as I tore it up. (Rip!) There goes that page. (Slash! Tear!) There go two more. Lots of people try to make a passing score on this. Then they arrive up here and see me ripping up the books and throwing the pages away. Some of them are offended; they get huffy. They say the whole business isn't fair. They've worked hard to be good, and they want cred-it, they say. I feel sorry for those people. But then there are the ones like you. When I begin to tear up your ledger book and throw away the pages listing your offenses, you stare at first in disbelief. But then you start laughing and giggling and crying because you realize the important thing isn't what you've done or not done, but who I am. I am Love—and you are Beloved. I kept your ledger book all these years just so that I could tear it up when we finally met face to face. You are the child of my heart. Welcome home, Beloved.*

The woman came to me a few more times, and I referred her to a counselor who helped her come to terms with the experiences in her earlier life that had blocked her from experiencing the love of God. Today she is a smiling, relaxed, increasingly radiant person.

It is not possible to live a Christian life, much less observe a holy Lent, without acknowledging at the outset that God loves us, along with everyone and everything else he has made. That is the beginning; the rest follows from it.

First Sunday in Lent

Led by the Spirit to Be Tempted

Almighty God, whose blessed Son was led by the Spirit to be tempted by Satan: Come quickly to help us who are assaulted by many temptations; and, as you know the weaknesses of each of us, let each one find you mighty to save.

All three synoptic Gospels agree that at the outset of his ministry, Jesus was tempted by Satan in the wilderness. They further agree that Jesus didn't just wander into the wilderness, but was led or driven by the Spirit to the place of temptation (Matthew 4:1; Mark 1:12; Luke 4:1). This seems at first like a grotesque parody of the truth. Why would the Spirit lead someone into the wilderness to be tempted? Has not Christ himself taught us to pray that we not be led into temptation?

This is one place where the new translation of the Lord's Prayer comes closer to the truth than the traditional text. The familiar "Lead us not into temptation" has been rendered in the official English ecumenical text, "Save us from the time of trial." No one is spared temptation. Temptation is part of being human, and God provides no means to sidestep it. We must face temptation head on, and if Jesus was to be fully human, he had to face it as well. The question is what we do when we face it.

The most trying time of temptation in my life came to me unexpectedly, which is perhaps usually the case with temptation. I thought I was doing well. But despite my seemingly successful career, I felt exhausted, alone, angry, abused, and trapped with no means of escape. I cried out to Christ (in whom I no longer really believed) to save me. My pain was not immediately lifted—perhaps Christ was waiting until my surrender was complete. But in time, Christ came to me, plucked me from the mire, embraced me, washed my soul, and gave me a new start I could never have dreamed of or asked for.

The temptation for me came in two phases. In the first phase, I vainly and naively accepted the very things Jesus had rejected in the wilderness: prestige, power, and possessions. These things are not bad in themselves, but they were bad for me because they began to corrode and consume my soul. The second phase of my temptation came when, having seen that the promise of happiness offered by these things was a false promise, I saw no way back from the darkness. The temptation was to sink into total despair. I nearly abandoned hope. But I clung to shreds of hope because the promises of Jesus were lodged in the recesses of my heart from long ago. I remembered them and claimed them.

Today I am a different man. Although my wilderness struggle with Satan was occasioned by my own decisions and behaviors, I also see that the Spirit of God was leading me, from the beginning to the end, even when I was unaware of the Spirit. God could not have made me a new man had the Spirit not led me into the wilderness to be tempted by Satan. The wilderness provided the occasion for Jesus to come to me and re-create me. But for my time in the wilderness, I would have known Jesus only in my mind, as someone I had read about and admired, but now I know him in my heart, as Master and Friend.

Julian of Norwich wrote: "He allows some of us to fall more heavily and more grievously than ever we did before, as it seems to us. And then we who are not all wise think that everything which we have undertaken was all nothing. But it is not so, for we need to fall, and we need to see it; for if we did not fall, we should not know how feeble and how wretched we are in ourselves, nor, too, should we know so completely the wonderful love of our Creator" (*Showings*, 61).

The struggle with temptation strengthens us, as exercise

strengthens the body, and purifies our souls for union with Christ. St. John of the Cross used the image of fire: "The soul is purged and prepared for union with the divine light just as fire acts upon a log in order to transform it into itself. Fire, when applied to wood, first dries it, driving out all moisture and causing it to shed any water it contains. Then it gradually turns the wood black, makes it dark and ugly, and even causes it to emit a bad odor. By drying out the wood, the fire brings to light and expels all those ugly and dark accidents which are contrary to fire. Finally, by heating and enkindling it from without, the fire transforms the wood into itself and makes it as beautiful as itself" (*Dark Night of the Soul*, 2. 10. 1).

SECOND SUNDAY IN LENT

All Who Have Gone Astray

O God, whose glory it is always to have mercy: Be gracious to all who have gone astray from your ways, and bring them again with penitent hearts and steadfast faith to embrace and hold fast the unchangeable truth of your Word.

This prayer is unique. All but five of the Collects for the Church Year are petitions for the church. Only five offer prayer for the world beyond the church. Three of the five pray for the conversion of the world, and one for its peaceable governance. This prayer stands alone in that its petition is not for the church, nor even for the world at large, but specifically for those who have rejected the gospel of Christ.

Why do people turn away from Christ? More often than we would like to admit, I suspect it is because of what they see in Christians: bickering, hypocrisy, arrogance, self-satisfaction, power struggles, money grubbing. When we Christians examine ourselves honestly, we see the same things. They are merely indications (along with other things perhaps not so visible to those outside) that we're in the right place, the place for shabby people who need cleaning up. We would do well to remind ourselves in our confessions that perhaps the main reason people turn aside from Jesus Christ is that they see so little of him in those who bear his name. It is well to pray for their conversion, but perhaps our conversion must come first.

The other reason people turn away from Christ has to do not with Christians, but with the people themselves. Those who have been abused, maligned, or exploited, who have not known human love, usually cannot accept the love of God. They become what they have known, often mocking what is good and holy. Although they are wrong to reject Christ, they are only partly to blame.

The words of this prayer are therefore gentle. There is no hint of rebuke or judgment. We remind ourselves that God is always merciful, as much to those who do not acknowledge him as to those who do. We then bid him be gracious to all who have gone astray, as he has been to us, bringing them, as he has brought us, to embrace the truth of his Word.

Christians sometimes try to do God's work for him. This prayer acknowledges that it is God who brings the wayward into the fold. We do not do this. We can introduce others to Christ and provide them opportunities to deepen their knowledge of him, but we must trust God to do the work of conversion in their lives. Our job is to live faithfully day to day and to make the church a place of welcome for those whom God brings in.

What of those who reject Christ and die without having returned to him? The devil dances with delight when we ask that sort of question. It is none of our business, and raising the question leads to fractious debates over who is in and who is out of the kingdom. Our energy wasted on such matters, we have little left with which to serve and enjoy our Lord. It is well to remember what this prayer affirms, that God's glory is *always* to have mercy and that the truth of his Word is *unchangeable*. I take this to mean that hell, which is the state of being separated from God by choice, is eternal only for those who choose to make it so. God's arms are eternally open to those who wish to return to him.

I recall having heard only two remarks on this subject that made sense to me. The first speaker said, "We need not worry about the fate of those who reject Christ, but we should perhaps be concerned about the fate of those whose failure to exhibit the love of Christ causes others to reject him." The second said, "We must leave the fate of those who reject Jesus Christ, as we leave all things, to the judgment and the mercy of God."

THIRD SUNDAY IN LENT

No Power in Ourselves

Almighty God, you know that we have no power in ourselves to help ourselves: Keep us both outwardly in our bodies and inwardly in our souls, that we may be defended from all adversities which may happen to the body, and from all evil thoughts which may assault and hurt the soul.

Alcoholics Anonymous was founded in 1935 by two men who had learned through repeated failures that they were powerless. Again and again they had tried and failed to control their drinking. Their health, marriages, careers, self-esteem—all was lost or about to be lost. Only when they finally admitted they were powerless did their recovery begin. Millions of people the world over, alcoholics and others, have received the gift of serenity through the Twelve Steps that began as a program of recovery for alcoholics and have since proved applicable to everyone. When references to alcohol are deleted, the first three steps of Alcoholics Anonymous become a concise statement of how anyone may begin the journey to spiritual health:

> *Step One:* We admitted we were powerless, that our lives had become unmanageable.

> *Step Two:* We came to believe that a Power greater than our- selves could restore us to sanity.

> *Step Three:* We made a decision to turn our will and our lives over to the care of God as we understood him.

Recovering alcoholics learn that their disease is more than a chemical addiction. For many, the chemical addiction proves easier to deal with than other parts of the disease. Addiction is primarily a spiritual malady, characterized by grandiosity, blaming of others, preoccupation with self, and grasping at control. It is a sickness of the will. After the chemical addiction has been tamed, the will must be redirected. This is a life-long process in which the alcoholic moves from strength to strength, from grace to grace.

One does not recover from alcoholism through strength of will. Alcoholics often possess enormous willpower, but the will is diseased, and the alcoholic's attempts to control his life through willpower must be abandoned before real recovery can begin. Only after one acknowledges one's helplessness and surrenders to the "Higher Power" can God enter the soul and begin to set things right.

This collect could be prayed at any Twelve Step recovery meet- ing or at any Christian worship service. It illustrates the profound coherence of Christian living with Twelve Step recovery principles. The prayer begins with the confession of our powerlessness, then asks God to protect us from both outward and inward dangers. Outward dangers, the "adversities which may happen to the body," include chemical addictions and other diseases. Inward dangers, the "evil thoughts which may assault and hurt the soul," are more subtle and destructive. They include the grandiose, self-preoccupied thoughts of the alcoholic and other disorientations of the will. In the Sermon on the Mount, Jesus says little about behavior, but concentrates instead on the health of the soul. All the Seven Deadly Sins of medieval Christendom are afflictions of the will: pride, avarice, envy, lust, anger, gluttony, and hopelessness. Taken together, the Seven Deadly Sins are a description both of addiction and of life apart from God.

FOURTH SUNDAY IN LENT

The True Bread

Gracious Father, whose blessed Son Jesus Christ came down from heaven to be the true bread which gives life to the world: Evermore give us this bread, that he may live in us, and we in him.

B read is a common, everyday food that has long symbolized all that is required to sustain life. To have bread is to live; to lack bread is to die.

Bread is also a common metaphor for what sustains the soul. The "bread of life" image has obvious eucharistic links, but its nuances extend into every aspect of a Christian's connections to Christ and to other believers.

We do not command grain to grow or understand how it grows. "The earth produces of itself, first the blade, then the ear, then the full grain in the ear" (Mark 4:28). The farmer knows that water and sunlight transform seed into grain, but he cannot know how this happens. He knows what to do, but the growth comes from elsewhere and the farmer does not control it.

For much of my life, I sought to nourish my own soul through what I read, thought, and did. My spiritual disciplines were intense. I kept a list of the devotional books I had read and practices I had mastered, almost as a gunslinger in the old West notched his belt for every person he had gunned down. I was going to become a spiritual master! It didn't work, of course. I had been trying to feed myself, according to my own diet. I eventually learned that the bread our souls long for comes only from Christ. Christ feeds his people—and he is himself the food he gives. The bread of life is not a teaching, a behavior, or a way of life to be mastered, any of which we could understand. It is a person. Our souls are nourished only through a relationship initiated, realized, and sustained from beyond ourselves. We live by receiving Christ into our souls.

The production of bread also requires us to depend on one another. Bread results from a communal effort, not a solo performance. Someone plants the seed, harvests the grain, separates the wheat from the chaff, grinds the flour, mixes and kneads the dough, bakes the bread, delivers it to the store, sells it, prepares it, and serves it—but the same person doesn't do all these things. Only when many individuals do their part is bread produced. I came to see that spiritual nurture depends on others as well. My early attempt to feed my soul by myself not only had no place for Christ, it also had no place for other people (except as authors). I finally came to see the foolishness of my effort when a few people who loved me confronted me with what they saw in me.

Nourishment is also a repeated, recurring act. Eating is not like inoculating. Once inoculated for smallpox, one need never think of it again. But when we eat a good supper in the evening, we still want breakfast in the morning, then lunch, and then supper again. I had thought that once I read a spiritual book or mastered a discipline, it would be mine, its wisdom filed in my mind for pulling out whenever I wanted to use it. I expect I thought of people that way as well. But it doesn't work like that. Certain spiritual texts and certain people have appeared in my life again and again. Each time, I encounter Christ in them, and each time, the encounter is fresh. It is because we have all changed: I have changed, the people have changed, and (to my mind, at least) the books and disciplines have changed. Every moment is an opportunity to be nourished again. Our inner selves, like our bodies, require repeated, regular sustenance; we must take and eat, again and again. Receiving the bread of life is part of the rhythm of Christian living, not a one-time-only infusion.

Finally, when bread is digested, its nutrients are passed into the bloodstream, which carries them to every cell of the body. The nutrients enter the cells to sustain and strengthen them. The bread actually *becomes* the cells it enters; it "indwells" the body. So also, the bread of life is not something that Christ merely brings and gives. Christ "indwells" the church and the souls of the faithful, "we in him and he in us." Christ "becomes our very life," as William Temple once said. By "indwelling" us, Christ extends the Incarnation, the Word made flesh, to include us all.

FIFTH SUNDAY IN LENT

Unruly Wills and Affections

Almighty God, you alone can bring into order the unruly wills and affections of sinners: Grant your people grace to love what you command and desire what you promise; that, among the swift and varied changes of the world, our hearts may surely there be fixed where true joys are to be found.

This is one of the most powerful prayers in the Book of Common Prayer. Its repeated couplets (wills and affections, love and desire, swift and varied, unruly wills and fixed hearts) suggest a soul in conflict with itself. We implore God to subdue our wandering, rebellious spirits. One can almost imagine St. Paul writing this prayer during his time of inner strife that he describes in Romans 7: "I do not understand my own actions. For I do not do what I want, but I do the very thing I hate . . . . Wretched man that I am! Who will deliver me from this body of death?"

We all experience such inner conflict. Our unruly wills and affections flit from one vanity to another, searching for joy in all the wrong places. Such searching saturates our hearts with desperation, emptiness, and fear. We become "rich in things and poor in soul," as Harry Emerson Fosdick expressed it. The joy we seek is found only in God. "Our hearts are restless until they find their rest in thee," as St. Augustine said. We pray in this collect that our hearts may be riveted to God so that, when our wills rebel once more, as they surely will, they may be held securely to the source of true joy.

The prayer asks that God cause us to love what he commands and desire what he promises. Even Christians often do not know what that is. Sometimes we think God commands certain behaviors, a list of do's and don'ts like the Ten Commandments. Or we think God commands us to do something for the spread of his kingdom, like build a church or raise a budget. But this is not what God commands. The Great Commandment is that we love God with all our heart and soul and mind, and our neighbor as ourselves. The commandment of God is not a list of behaviors or accomplishments but a relationship. God commands us to love him and promises to love us. To love what God commands and desire what he promises is to rest in the love of God.

The prayer is realistic about human nature. It does not ask that God enable us to do as he commands by strengthening our wills—to strengthen the human will would only be to deepen its rebellion. Nor does the prayer ask that God strengthen our higher self that it may prevail over our lower self. It says nothing about what we are to do, because it is not in our power to do what needs doing. The prayer asks that God assert his power to grasp and reorder our wills and affections. This was what John Donne asked of God in an often quoted sonnet:

> Batter my heart, three-person'd God; for you
> As yet but knock; breathe, shine, and seek to mend;
> That I may rise, and stand, o'erthrow me, and bend
> Your force, to break, blow, burn, and make me new.
> I, like an usurp'd town, to another due,
> Labour to admit you, but O, to no end.
> Reason, your viceroy in me, me should defend,
> But is captived, and proves weak or untrue,
> Yet dearly I love you, and would be loved fain,
> But am betroth'd unto your enemy;
> Divorce me, untie, or break that knot again,
> Take me to you, imprison me, for I,
> Except you enthrall me, never shall be free,
> Nor ever chaste, except you ravish me.

God commands, and God must give what he commands. Our part is simply to submit, to surrender and let God be God in our lives. The prophet Jeremiah envisioned such a conversion for Judah following the Exile: "I will put my law within them, and I will write it upon their hearts; and I will be their God, and they shall be my people. And no longer shall each man teach his neighbor and each his brother saying, 'Know the Lord,' for they shall all know me, from the least of them to the greatest, says the Lord" (Jeremiah 31:33–34).

The result will be hearts fixed where true joys are to be found. They are found only in the arms of God.

S<small>UNDAY OF THE</small> P<small>ASSION</small>: P<small>ALM</small> S<small>UNDAY</small>

His Great Humility

Almighty and everliving God, in your tender love for the human race you sent your Son our Savior Jesus Christ to take upon him our nature, and to suffer death upon the cross, giving us the example of his great humility: Mercifully grant that we may walk in the way of his suffering, and also share in his resurrection.

This collect comes close to being a miniature creed. All the major themes of the classical creeds are present or implied in this brief prayer: The salutation addresses God as almighty and everliving, suggesting his role as Creator and Sustainer of the universe. The opening clause affirms the doctrine of the Incarnation and points to the crucifixion. The petition asks that we may share both in Christ's suffering and in his resurrection victory.

The prayer also mentions something that, though implied in the creeds, is not explicitly stated—the humility of Christ. The mention of humility adds interpretative color to the creeds, flesh to the doctrinal skeleton. Humility is not a sign of weakness, an abandoning of the self to suffering, betrayal, and abuse because the identity of the abused is surrendered to that of the abuser. Some people mistake such weakness for humility. Real humility flows from a strength so secure that maintaining control and getting one's way cease to matter. The humble person sees things as they really are, knows what is most important, what is important, and what is not important, acting out of the security such knowledge affords. He often puts others ahead of himself, not out of weakness, but out of strength, not because he is compelled to, but because he chooses to.

I shall never forget an incident that occurred during my first year in seminary. I lived in a large, old rooming house, with several other students. Fred was one of them. Fred was a Jew, the only Jew in the student body of this Christian school. He had enrolled there because he wanted to learn anything Christians could teach him about his God. Fred meticulously observed all the holy days and teachings of conservative Judaism. One of those teachings forbade the eating of pork. Fred never made a big deal out of this when he was with us, but we knew he was careful to avoid pork in any form.

Our landlady was a vicious woman who hated Jews. One evening she invited all her renters for supper. The entree was baked ham. Bacon had been crumbled over the salad. The green beans had been simmering all day in fatback. A strip of bacon lay across the twice-baked potato. Our landlady delighted in heaping Fred's plate with these foods. The rest of us could hardly believe what we were seeing. The entire occasion, it became clear to us, had been designed to embarrass and trick Fred.

We didn't know what to do. It was up to Fred, I finally decided. I watched him. Fred ate every bite on his plate, and after the meal thanked his hostess for her kindness and graciousness in inviting him to dinner. Later that night we asked Fred why he had broken his usual discipline and eaten pork. "The most important commandment in my religion is to love God and my neighbor," he said. "Dietary laws are important, but love is more important. Part of loving my neighbor is always to think the best of my neighbor and to accept hospitality graciously offered."

When I think of the humility of Christ, I often think of Fred. I don't know whether Fred learned anything about his God from us that year, but I learned something about my God from Fred. That one night forty years ago, I saw Jesus Christ in a young, unconverted, unbaptized Jew in an old Tennessee rooming house.

MONDAY IN HOLY WEEK

The Way of the Cross

Almighty God, whose most dear Son went not up to joy but first he suffered pain, and entered not into glory before he was crucified: Mercifully grant that we, walking in the way of the cross, may find it none other than the way of life and peace.

The fundamental paradox of Christian living is that one must die before one can live. St. Paul speaks of baptism as being buried with Christ in order that we may be raised with him (Romans 6:4; Colossians 2:12), and Jesus says in St. John's Gospel that "unless a grain of wheat falls into the earth and dies, it remains alone; but if it dies, it bears much fruit. He who loves his life loses it, and he who hates his life in this world will keep it for eternal life" (John 12:24–25).

The grain of wheat falling into the earth is not the only metaphor Christian thinkers have suggested to illustrate this truth: unless the worm leaves the security of the cocoon, it cannot become a butterfly; unless the leaves fall from the trees and enrich the ground, the new growth of spring will not follow. Helpful as such analogies are, this truth, I believe, can be learned only through personal experience; the way of the cross carries little meaning *for me* until *I myself* learn what it is to die.

The way of the cross is the acceptance of our neediness and dependence. It includes acknowledging physical death but is primarily an experience of the soul, often occasioned by some failure or suffering that humbles us. Our grandiose, ambitious schemes

come crashing down around us and we find ourselves lying amid
the smoldering ashes of our dreams. Then we realize that our
dreams were spun out of air, that they were not of God, but of
ourselves, and that they never mattered because only what is of
God matters. God gives new life when, usually as the result of
failure or suffering, the old self dies. St. Paul commented that "our
old self was crucified with him . . . . If we have died with Christ,
we believe that we shall also live with him" (Romans 6:6, 8), and
urged his churches to put off their old nature (Ephesians 4:22) and
to put on the new (Colossians 3:10). Teilhard de Chardin
described the way of the cross:

> Such in fact, is the Christian estimate, paradoxical though
> it be, of suffering: not only is evident, tangible failure
> classed as accidental mishap, but it can even be regarded as
> preferable to actual success, on the ground that failure
> offers a wider basis for sanctification than success. No
> doctrine is more eminently in harmony with the teaching
> of the Gospels than the primacy of humility and suffering.
> There can be no possible doubt but that Christ took the
> road of abnegation, detachment and renunciation, and that
> his disciples must follow him. The road along which his
> kingdom makes progress is the way of relinquishment, of
> blood and tears—the way of the Cross. (*The Prayer of the
> Universe*, Perennial Library edition [New York: Harper and
> Row, 1965; revised 1973], 86)

Should we, then, seek suffering? Certainly not. Setting out to
suffer would not bring us closer to God, for it would not teach
humility. We might congratulate ourselves on having succeeded at
suffering. We are created to become all that God envisions us
becoming, but it seems a universal flaw in the human character
that we seek the satisfaction of our desires rather than the will of
God. Failure and suffering bring us to our senses.

I have heard many recovering alcoholics and drug addicts say
how grateful they are to be alcoholics and drug addicts. They do

not mean that addiction is a good thing: addiction is a spiritual prison, and recovering people are grateful to have been freed from it. But the recovering addict also realizes that it wasn't until his life began to crumble that he acknowledged his wretchedness and turned to God. If that had not happened, he might never have known the joy of an intimate relationship with his "Higher Power," and for that reason, he is grateful to have become an alcoholic or addict.

Perhaps some few surrender the will without losing anything at all. For most of us, though, a humbling experience of failure or suffering is required. But failure and suffering by no means invariably lead to surrender of the will. They can also reinforce the old self's inflated ego by adding bitterness and resentment to the picture, and that of course does not lead to new life. Surrender of the will is the essential thing—that is what it means to be crucified with Christ, to walk the way of the cross. We do not choose what the way of the cross will mean for us. It is given to us; by accepting what is given, we gain what we never knew to ask for.

TUESDAY IN HOLY WEEK

Glory in the Cross

O God, by the passion of your blessed Son you made an instrument of shameful death to be for us the means of life: Grant us so to glory in the cross of Christ, that we may gladly suffer shame and loss for the sake of your Son our Savior Jesus Christ.

The chief visual symbol of the Christian faith is a simple geometric figure consisting of two lines intersecting at a right angle. Artists have created thousands of variations on this basic design. Some of these may be seen above the piano in my study, where a large frame hangs on the wall, displaying nearly a hundred crosses, most just an inch or two tall. My wife and I have bought a cross to remember our trip when we've traveled to a new destination, and friends have brought them to us as gifts. Some of these crosses are ornate, some simple; a few are valuable, most are inexpensive. They are made of stone, metal, fabric, glass, paper, sticks, clay, bones, wire, coal, leather, lace, plastic, wood. I love this collection of crosses, because of the people and places I associate with it and because of its aesthetic appeal to me, but mostly because of what the cross signifies.

Crosses appear in many places: on steeples, behind altars, on the front of prayer books, around people's necks, in lapels, on bumper stickers and billboards. But a more unlikely symbol for a religion could hardly be imagined. We have so beautified the cross as nearly to rob it of its meaning. The cross is, first of all, a horrible thing, an instrument of torture and execution. It is in the same class with the electric chair and the hangman's noose. Imagine walking into church to find that the cross behind the altar had been replaced by an electric chair with its headcap, wires, belts, and straps. How odd that such a thing is so widely venerated!

But venerated it is, and this has been the case from earliest Christian times. "Far be it from me to glory except in the cross of our Lord Jesus Christ," St. Paul wrote (Galatians 6:14). It is not the fact of an execution that has endeared the cross to Christians of all ages—millions of people have been executed before and since. Nor is it the fact of Christ's innocence—other innocent people have died. Christians glory in the cross because we see the love of God poured out upon it and flowing from it to embrace all things.

The cross is a terrible thing if we see it as an instrument of torture only, and it is especially terrible if we see it as the instrument of torture demanded by a raging God who could be satisfied only by the blood of an innocent victim. But we do not think of the cross as something that changed God's disposition toward us, but as something that revealed God's disposition toward us. "The cross did not change God's mind; it expressed it," wrote John Coburn. "The cross turns everything around. God does not *demand* that we love him. He places that demand upon himself. Only he can meet that demand. And he does. This is how much he loves us—so much that he dies for us. . . . He is not making demands upon us through his Son. He is making love to us" (*A Life to Live, A Way to Pray*, p. 119, italics in original).

When the seventeenth-century poet Thomas Traherne gazed upon the cross, he saw a vision of love calling all of creation to itself:

> The cross is the abyss of wonders, the centre of desires, the school of virtues, the house of wisdom, the throne of love, the theater of joys, and the place of sorrows; it is the root of happiness and the gate of heaven. . . . It is the most exalted of all objects. It is an ensign lifted up for all nations. . . . The dispersed of Judah shall be gathered together to it, from the four corners of the earth. . . . All eyes and hearts may convert and turn unto this object, cleave unto this centre, and by it enter into rest. . . . There we might see all nations assembled with their eyes and hearts upon it. There we may see God's goodness, wisdom, and power, yea, his mercy and anger displayed. There we may see man's sin and infinite value, his hope and fear, his misery and happiness. There we might see the Rock of Ages, and the joys of heaven. . . . There we may see the most distant things in eternity united: all mysteries at once couched together and explained. . . . It is a well of life beneath in which we may see the face of heaven above: and the only mirror, wherein all things appear in their proper colors, that is, sprinkled in the Blood of our Lord and Savior. The cross of Christ is the Jacob's ladder by which we ascend into the highest heavens. There we see joyful patriarchs, expecting saints, and prophets ministering,

apostles publishing, and doctors teaching, all nations concentering, and angels praising. That cross is a tree set on fire with invisible flame, that illuminateth all the world. The flame is love. (*Centuries of Meditations*, I, 58—60)

WEDNESDAY IN HOLY WEEK

Grace to Accept

Lord God, whose blessed Son our Savior gave his body to be whipped and his face to be spit upon: Give us grace to accept joyfully the sufferings of the present time, confident of the glory that shall be revealed.

Human suffering is caused by three things. The first is events in nature: earthquakes, storms, physical illnesses, death, and so on. God could have created a world without such things, but it would have been an enormously different world from the one we live in. Rocks falling in an avalanche would stop half-way down the mountain if a village lay below; a deadly virus would be rendered inert just as it entered our lungs; tornados and hurricanes would bypass populated areas; the aging process would stop when we reached the prime of life. Such a world would have no laws of nature because nature would be forever adjusting her ways so as to inflict no pain. There would be no sciences because there would be no enduring structures to investigate. The sole purpose of such a world would be to maximize human pleasure, and that, clearly, is not the purpose God had in mind when he created our world.

The second cause of human suffering is the cruelty of people to each other. Cruelty ranges from tiny offenses such as gossiping and thoughtlessness to global holocausts. This prayer refers to Jesus' suffering as a result of human cruelty in mentioning that he was whipped and spit upon. God could have created beings incapable of cruelty to one another, but we would have been enormously different creatures than we are, rather like robots or computers. Robots and computers lack free will; they do what they are programmed to do, and while they are useful, it is not possible to form a loving relationship with a being that lacks free will. God endowed human beings with free will because he seeks to draw us into a loving relationship with him. This necessarily includes the possibility of evil as well as good.

The third cause of human suffering is the games we play with ourselves in our minds. This suffering is self-inflicted. Our lives are not as we would like them to be: other people misunderstand us, take us for granted, don't give us what we deserve, make unreasonable demands of us, gossip about us, break their promises to us, mistreat and abuse us, have more money, friends, and influence than we—all of which leads us to feel sorry for ourselves. We fill our minds with false statements such as: "I'm an innocent victim. Other people are bad while I am good. I'm not responsible for what happens to me. I'm different and better than other people. My wants are entirely reasonable. I should not have to put up with unpleasant realities. I'm entitled to a life of seamless happiness." The result of repeating such falsehoods to ourselves is consuming jealousy, bitterness, resentment, and anger. It is self-will eroding our spiritual health as it poisons our relationships with God and other people. Self-will is always possible in a creature whose creator has endowed it with free will.

The alternative is acceptance. We can begin by accepting the world as it is. We often do not like living in a world with limits and natural laws, but we can learn to accept it. Life is like a game with fixed rules. In baseball, fair territory is defined by the foul lines, the distance between bases is ninety feet, and the strike zone is the area above home plate and between the batter's knees and shoulders. We may or may not like these rules. At times, we would prefer that fair territory be expanded or constricted, the bases be moved closer together or farther apart, the strike zone enlarged or shrunk. But the rules are what they are, and if we would play the game, we must accept the rules and play by them. Blaming those who wrote the rule book for our poor play will only add to our suffering and that of others who must listen to our complaining.

We also do not like everything that other people do. We can grumble and feel sorry for ourselves, or we can accept reality, including the suffering that is part of human relationships. Among the realities we may have to accept are our imperfect marriage, dead-end job, unruly children, judgmental parents, and unreliable friends and colleagues. Usually we can do something to improve the relationships that cause us suffering, but some things are beyond our power to change. Acceptance means knowing what we can change and what we cannot change. As the famous prayer says, "God, grant me the serenity to accept the things I cannot change, to change the things I can, and the wisdom to know the difference."

We must also accept ourselves, including our own part in creating our suffering and inflicting suffering on others. We are not innocent victims, but fellow-perpetrators of cruelty. We malign others as often as others malign us, and much of the suffering we experience results from our own misbehavior and ill will and the lies we tell ourselves. We cannot begin to experience healing and renewal until we acknowledge that we need it.

This prayer asks that we may "accept joyfully the sufferings of the present time." Joyful acceptance of suffering does not mean that we must like it. The key to joyful acceptance, even of suffering, is to find God in every moment. There is no circumstance, no place, no person, no thought, feeling, or experience, where God does not dwell. If we look, we will find God in all things. The question is not whether God is there, but whether we acknowledge his presence.

MAUNDY THURSDAY

The Sacrament of His Body and Blood

Almighty Father, whose dear Son, on the night before he suffered, instituted the Sacrament of his Body and Blood: Mercifully grant that we may receive it thankfully in remembrance of Jesus Christ our Lord, who in these holy mysteries gives us a pledge of eternal life.

On the night before he died, Jesus shared a supper with his disciples, during which he took bread, blessed it, broke it, and gave it to the disciples with the words, "This is my body; this is my blood." Jesus then commanded his disciples to "do this in remembrance of me."

"Was ever another command so obeyed?" asked Dom Gregory Dix in a famous passage at the end of his book *The Shape of the Liturgy*:

For century after century, spreading slowly to every continent and country and among every race on earth, this action has been done, in every conceivable human circumstance, for every conceivable human need from infancy and before it to extreme old age and after it, from the pinnacles of earthly greatness to the refuge of fugitives in the caves and dens of the earth. Men have found no better thing than this to do for kings at their crowning and for criminals going to the scaffold; for armies in triumph or for a bride and bridegroom in a little country church; for the proclamation of a dogma or for a good crop of wheat; for the wisdom of the Parliament of a mighty nation or for a sick old woman afraid to die; for a schoolboy sitting for an examination or for Columbus setting out to discover America; for the famine of whole provinces or for the soul of a dead lover; in thankfulness because my father did not die of pneumonia; for a village headman much tempted to return to fetish because the yams had failed; because the Turk was at the gates of Vienna; for the repentance of Margaret; for the settlement of a strike; for a son for a barren woman; for Captain so-and-so, wounded and prisoner of war; while the lions roared in the nearby amphitheater; on the beach at Dunkirk; while the hiss of scythes in the thick June grass came faintly through the windows of the church; tremulously, by an old monk on the fiftieth anniversary of his vows; furtively, by an exiled bishop who had hewn timber all day in a prison camp near Murmansk; gorgeously, for the canonization of St. Joan of Arc—one could fill many pages with the reasons why men have done this, and not tell a hundredth part of them. And best of all, week by week and month by month, on a hundred thousand successive Sundays, faithfully, unfailingly, across all the parishes of Christendom, the pastors have done this just to make the plebs sancta Dei—the holy common people of God.

I have been known to drive for an hour while on vacation to get to the nearest church on Sunday in order to partake of this meal. Friends and family members have occasionally asked why I do this, and I am unable to answer. It defies explaining.

On the same night Jesus shared this supper with his disciples, he prayed to his Father that the disciples and those who would come after them might "be one even as we are one, I in them and thou in me, that they may become perfectly one" (John 17:22–23). But far from becoming the sacrament of unity that Christ intended, this simple meal has been one of the chief causes of division and suspicion among Christians through the centuries. We cannot seem to agree what exactly it is that we do in remembrance of our Lord. Volumes have been written on this question, churches have broken into schism over it, and martyrs have been burned at the stake when their opinion differed from the accepted view.

Jesus commanded his followers to *do* this in his memory, not to *understand* it. We tell our young children to eat their vegetables but do not expect them to understand the principles of nutrition, and when they ask why they should eat their vegetables, we may say, "Because I say so." Sometimes it is necessary simply to do as we are told when we cannot understand, because we trust the one issuing the command. Only the intellectually arrogant pretend to understand what is beyond their comprehension. The very attempt at explanation threatens to rob the meal of its mystery and power. Only when obedience becomes more important to the church than understanding will all Christians gather around a common table, in thanksgiving for blessings that can be received but never comprehended.

Some of those who came before us also realized that this meal was given to us to be received, not understood. Queen Elizabeth I, who reigned during a time of fractious debate over the meaning of sacraments, is said to have written a clever and often-quoted verse on the subject:

Christ was the word that spake it,
He took the bread and brake it;
And what his words did make it,
This I believe and take it.

Richard Hooker, writing at the same time, expressed the same truth in more lofty terms:

Let it therefore be sufficient for me presenting myself at the Lord's table to know what there I receive from him, without searching or inquiring of the manner how Christ performeth his promise; let disputes and questions, enemies to piety, abatements of true devotion, and hitherto in

this cause but over-patiently heard, let them take their
rest . . . what these elements are in themselves it skilleth
not, it is enough that to me which take them they are the
body, and blood of Christ, his promise in witness hereof
sufficeth, his word he knoweth which way to accomplish;
why should any cogitation possess the mind of a faithful
communicant but this, O my God thou art true, O my
Soul thou art happy? (*Of the Laws of Ecclesiastical Polity*,
V, lxvii, 12)

GOOD FRIDAY

Behold This Your Family

*Almighty God, we pray you graciously to behold this your
family, for whom our Lord Jesus Christ was willing to be
betrayed, and given into the hands of sinners, and to suffer
death upon the cross.*

This prayer asks Jesus, bleeding from the cross, to look at us.
The words "your family" can be taken to mean the church,
those baptized into fellowship with Christ, or the world, those
whom Christ loves. For our purposes on this day, it does not
matter. Christ is looking at us as his strength ebbs away. What does
he see?

He sees us keeping busy. We can't take too much time over this
execution because we have payrolls to meet, bills and taxes to pay,
appointments to keep, equipment to repair, floors to mop, sched-

ules to consult, letters to write, phone calls to return, books to publish, products to make, deliver, and sell. We have businesses, factories, schools, agencies, churches, hospitals to run, and we can't allow these things to come to a halt. It's unfortunate that this innocent man has been tried and convicted, but we have work to do and must leave questions of jurisprudence to others. Jesus looks down from the cross and sees his family carrying on as usual.

He sees us capitalizing on him. Here's an opportunity. Someone must cook and set the tables for these out-of-town guests who have come for the Passover. Someone must manage the crowd. Someone must run the souvenir stands that sell trinkets, T-shirts with his picture on them, videotapes of the trial. Someone must organize the tour groups, the seminars, the press conferences. Someone must host the talk shows. Someone must arrange the flowers, prepare the altar, duplicate the bulletins. Jesus looks down from the cross and sees his family creating a burlesque out of his suffering.

He sees us mocking. Some shout, "He saved others; let him save himself, if he is the Christ of God, his Chosen One! If you are the King of the Jews, save yourself!" (Luke 23:35, 37). He had his head in the clouds, we snicker. All that love-your-enemies-and-turn-the-other-cheek stuff sounds nice in Sunday school, but look where it leads you! You better know how the world really operates if you want to get ahead in life. We could have told him if he would have listened to us! Jesus looks down from the cross and sees his family scoffing at him.

He sees us confused. The mockers are right—he did save others. Now we hear them taunting him to save himself—why does he not do it? Have we been mistaken to trust and follow him? What does all this mean, and where do we turn now? When he said we were forgiven, did it amount to nothing after all? Is the whole thing a hoax? Jesus looks down from the cross and sees his family groping in the dark.

He sees us betraying him. Judas is the most notorious of Jesus' betrayers because his act was overt and pivotal. But he is not the only betrayer among Jesus' friends. Peter denied Jesus three times when he could have stood by him. And what about us—where are we? Scampering away, perhaps hanging around the fringe of the crowd where we can remain anonymous. Jesus looks down from the cross and sees his family, nervously shuffling our feet, wringing our hands.

He sees us weeping. We know what we have done. Jesus bleeds on the cross because of our inertia, duplicity, cowardice, pettiness, and self-centeredness. Remorse overwhelms us. The time to act has passed and we stand idly by now, helplessly watching the events that we might have stopped had we acted earlier. We are responsible; we have done this; we have offended. Jesus looks down from the cross and sees his family crying over good deeds left undone.

Jesus beholds his family. What does he say?

HOLY SATURDAY

Await with Him

O God, Creator of heaven and earth: Grant that, as the crucified body of your dear Son was laid in the tomb and rested on this holy Sabbath, so we may await with him the coming of the third day, and rise with him to newness of life.

This is the day of waiting in the dark for what may never come.

All has been lost: loved ones, friends, work, play, the past, the future, vitality, feeling, caring. Drained dry, Jesus lies motionless in the silent cave. Even the pain is gone. All is gone.

We wait with Jesus for the coming of the third day. But there is no confidence in the promise of the third day, for confidence is part of what has been lost. There is nothing but waiting for what may never come. This is the moment of pure passivity, of sheer nothingness.

I have experienced moments of what I thought was nothingness. But I was wrong—I have never seen the inside of the tomb. Few people of my age have, I suspect. But I think that in some limited way, my paternal grandmother saw it. She was 101 years old when she died in a Kentucky nursing home. When I visited her toward the end, she did not know who I was or who she was. She had lost everything except the present moment and the savings my grandfather had left her fifteen years earlier—and she had lost the awareness even of that.

A few years earlier, my grandmother still clung to shreds of who she was. She was sadder then. "There can hardly be a more alienating feeling than that which believes, 'I am who I was,'" wrote Henri Nouwen (*Aging*, p. 40). My grandmother moved beyond that. When I saw her near the end, there was no future for her, only the present, and in some strange way, the distant past, which had returned to become part of her present.

Although she had her fitful moments (which her nurses and my mother, who visited her daily, valiantly coped with), more often, my grandmother waited patiently, passively, expecting nothing. This was something she had never done before. For most of her life, my grandmother had been a strong-willed, dominating woman, never content, always pressing to impress her convictions on her children and grandchildren. But now, for the first time in her life, she was, at least occasionally, content simply to be and to let others be. Outside my grandmother's window stood a bird feeder, visited by robins, sparrows, and finches. My grandmother rediscovered this feeder several times each day and remarked, to no one in particular, "Look! There are birds outside my window!"

I don't know why God allowed my grandmother to continue so long in this life. Although her heart still beat and her lungs inhaled, she seemed to me, in many ways, already to have died. She sat in her room peering into the tomb, into sheer nothingness. In a limited way, I glimpsed the face of Jesus, silently waiting in the tomb on this holy Sabbath, when I gazed into my grandmother's vacant eyes. She had glimpsed the inside of that tomb, where all is lost. And she had discovered that it need not terrify.

Despite her limited awareness of her identity and surroundings, during her final years my grandmother seemed to accept the fact that she could no longer achieve, control, or direct. She did not articulate this, of course, and years earlier, when she did speak, abandonment of control was not what she talked about. But if death is the ultimate act of surrender into the arms of God, my grandmother seemed to find a place in those arms. Her condition, though distressing to those who cared for her, seemed to grow less distressing to her. At long last and for the first time in her life, I think she had learned to wait.

I am certain my grandmother never read the prayer for use by a sick person in the morning, on page 461 of the Episcopal Book of Common Prayer, but I thought of that prayer when I sat with her near the end: "This is another day, O Lord. I know not what it will bring forth, but make me ready, Lord, for whatever it may be. If I am to stand up, help me to stand bravely. If I am to sit still, help me to sit quietly. If I am to lie low, help me to do it patiently. And if I am to do nothing, let me do it gallantly. Make these words more than words, and give me the Spirit of Jesus."

Out of this passivity, meaning somehow emerges. Again, Henri Nouwen:

> We, too, must move from action to "passion," from being in control to being dependent, from taking initiatives to having to wait, from living to dying. Painful and nearly impossible as this move seems to be, it is in this movement that our true fruitfulness is hidden. . . . It is not easy to trust that our lives will bear fruit through this sort of dependence because, for the most part, we ourselves experience dependence as uselessness and as burdensome. . . . Believing that our lives come to fulfillment in dependence requires a tremendous leap of faith. Everything that we see or feel and everything that our society suggests to us

through the values and ideas it holds up to us point in the opposite direction. . . . The well-known words of the apostle Paul, "God chose those who by human standards are weak to shame the strong" (1 Corinthians 1:27), take on new meaning here because the weak are not only the poor, the disabled, and the mentally ill, but also the dying—and all of us will be dying one day. We must trust that it is also in *this* weakness that God shames the strong and reveals true human fruitfulness. (*Our Greatest Gift*, pp. 92–94, italics in original)

Was my grandmother's "fruitfulness" manifest as she sat at her window gazing absently at the birds? Was the "fruitfulness" of Jesus' life manifest by his lying motionless in the silent cave? And will the third day come? Nouwen is right—it "requires a tremendous leap of faith." Part of the tomb's darkness is that while we may remember the promise of the third day, we cannot know whether the promise will come true. There is only one thing left to do: wait with Jesus.

Easter Season

. ❦ .

EASTER DAY

The Joy of His Resurrection

O God, who for our redemption gave your only-begotten Son to the death of the cross, and by his glorious resurrection delivered us from the power of our enemy: Grant us so to die daily to sin, that we may evermore live with him in the joy of his resurrection.

Opening with a reference to the cross and concluding with the joy of the resurrection, this prayer has been called a "fitting transition" from Lent to Easter. The cross is the emblem of evil, of justice flouted. As I write these words, the lead news stories come from Iraq, Somalia, Afghanistan, the Sudan, and Gaza, all places where innocent people suffer and evil seems to reign. How can anyone read the newspaper or watch television and seriously speak of having been "delivered . . . from the power of our enemy?" Everywhere in the world, the paltry powers that challenge our enemy seem woeful and helpless.

Only those who become like little children can celebrate the joy of the resurrection. Somewhere between childhood and adulthood, most of us stopped believing in dreams and fairy tales. We started believing instead in the headlines and nightly newscasts. Somebody told us that was the "real world," and that the name of the game was power. We believed it.

But the Bible laughs at power. Suffering is not glossed over, but borne, and then transcended. Glory shines in weakness and surrender. The deepest biblical truths are expressed in dreams and fairy tales—which only children believe in. Perhaps this is what Jesus meant when he said that unless we turn and become like children, we will never enter the kingdom of heaven (Matthew 18:3). Easter is the day for people, of whatever age, who see through the headlines to the reality of fairy tales, who believe in dreams come true.

In dreams, fairy tales, and Bible stories, adult reality is turned upside down; the world's order is reversed: the pompous emperor is revealed as a naked fool when a child sees what its elders had not seen; the sister relegated to the role of charwoman becomes the queen of the ball; the princess falls in love with a frog and the frog turns out to be a prince. Even our American political mythology revels in fortunes reversed: refugees found what will become a great nation; a boy born in a log cabin reaches the White House and saves that nation.

The Bible is full of the same thing: unworthy Jacob fathers the people of God; the brother sold into slavery lives to save those who sold him; slaves fleeing their oppressors find a promised land flowing with milk and honey; the young boy who tended the sheep is chosen king over his warrior brothers.

This theme is central in the life and teachings of Jesus as well: Lazarus is comforted in the bosom of Abraham while Dives gasps for water; street people are welcomed into the wedding feast; the prodigal son is received home with a ring, new shoes, and a party; "He hath put down the mighty from their seat, and hath exalted the humble and meek" (Luke 1:52). And of course the biggest reversal of all: the innocent victim nailed to the cross rises from the dead.

This is, of course, all foolishness. Everyone knows fairy tales don't come true. Or do they? Does *everyone* know that fairy tales don't come true? Young children suspect they might. Could the children be right? Can we believe the Bible? Or is what we see on the nightly news all there is? Is the resurrection just a big joke?

That's exactly what it is. The resurrection of Jesus is the biggest joke of all, and the most hilarious thing about it is that it's true. "Easter is the beginning of the laughter of the redeemed and the dance of the liberated and the creative game of fantasy. Since earliest times Easter hymns have celebrated the victory of life by laughing at death, by mocking hell, and by making the lords of this world absurd," Jürgen Moltmann has said (*Experiences of God*, pp. 32–33).

Jesus appeared to the disciples in a closed room on Easter night, gave them his peace, and showed them his hands and his side. The disciples were "glad" when they saw him (John 20:20). What sort of gladness was this? I suspect the disciples giggled and cackled like children, slapping their knees and poking each other in the ribs; they had just witnessed the ultimate punch line.

Easter is for everyone, but not everyone gets the picture. Some see only what the world sees. But some see beyond the world. Children are more likely to get it than adults. Clowns get it. Artists often get it. People who hug and sing loud in church have probably got it.

The Easter acclamation is: "Alleluia. Christ is risen." The response: "The Lord is risen indeed. Alleluia." Say it laughing.

THAT SPIRIT OF ADOPTION

O God, who made this most holy night to shine with the glory of the Lord's resurrection: Stir up in your Church that Spirit of adoption which is given to us in Baptism, that we, being renewed both in body and mind, may worship you in sincerity and truth.

My wife's mother was adopted as an infant. She grew up as Virginia Schaub, the only child of the local butcher and mayor of a small town in northern Michigan. Ginny always knew she had been adopted. She also knew that her biological mother was a local person, living in the same community, a town small enough that everyone knew everyone else. But she didn't know who her biological parents were and never cared to know.

For years I could not understand my mother-in-law's indifference to her biological roots. "Weren't you curious to know whether you had any brothers and sisters going through school at the same time you were, possibly even among your friends and playmates?" I asked.

"I don't have any brothers and sisters; I am an only child," she said. That seemed to end the matter.

Ginny was fifty years old when I met her. I later learned that at some point during her young adult years, she had inadvertently come across the identity of her biological mother. That she had learned this information emerged one day, years later, in a conversation with my wife and me. Ginny mentioned it in passing, as an aside while discussing something else, and then moved on to other topics, treating the matter as of no consequence. My wife and I stared at her. "So you know who your mother was! What kind of woman was she?" we asked eagerly.

"Oh, she was a young woman who got pregnant out of wedlock and gave me up for adoption. She later married and had several other children," Ginny said.

"So you've got half-brothers and sisters living right there in town with you! Who are they? What kind of people are they?"

"They're nice enough people. I knew them when I was growing up, but they were younger than me in school and I didn't know them well. I still pass them on the street from time to time. I don't know whether they know I'm their half-sister or not. It doesn't matter. My parents were Clarence and Iva Schaub, and I'm their only child." That really did end the matter.

Ginny's confident, un-self-conscious identification with her adopted parents serves as a model for a Christian's identity with his heavenly Father. We are by nature different from God: God is Creator— omnipotent, omniscient, infinite, eternal; we are creatures—weak, ignorant, limited, mortal. By nature, we inhabit a realm vastly different from that of God. Our nature determines certain things about us, just as a person's genes determine her stature, features, and biological predispositions. But our identity is something else, determined by the One who has chosen and loved us. We are children of God by adoption and grace (as one of the Christmas collects says), and it is that fact that defines our true identity.

Baptism often takes place on Easter Eve, for which this prayer is most appropriate. Our baptism is the seal of our adoption by God into his family and household—our baptismal certificate is, as it were, our adoption paper. In this collect we pray that the Spirit of adoption, given to us in baptism, be stirred up in the church. Unlike my mother-in-law, we in the church often forget who we are and act as if we are still part of the household into which we were born. But our adoption is final and irrevocable; we will always belong to God. When we pray that God renew us "both in body and mind" that we may worship him "in sincerity and truth," we ask him to give us the confidence and security that come from knowing our real identity.

THE GATE OF EVERLASTING LIFE

Almighty God, who through your only-begotten Son Jesus Christ overcame death and opened to us the gate of everlasting life: Grant that we, who celebrate with joy the day of the Lord's resurrection, may be raised from the death of sin by your life-giving Spirit.

The gate or door is a common image in spiritual writing, signifying transition in the soul. The image of the pearly gates in heaven, a common feature in cartoonists' depictions of the next life, comes from scripture (Revelation 21:21). The Episcopal burial office prays that the deceased may pass "through the grave and gate of death" (Book of Common Prayer, p. 480). In allegorical and fantasy literature as well, the gate or door signifies transition from one world into another. The door to hell in Dante's *Inferno* bears the terrifying message, "Abandon hope all ye who enter here." Christian passes through the Wicket Gate on his way to the Celestial Kingdom in John Bunyan's *The Pilgrim's Progress*. The wardrobe door in C. S. Lewis's *The Lion, the Witch, and the Wardrobe* is the point of entry into Narnia.

This prayer affirms that Christ has "opened to us the gate of everlasting life." What is this gate?

A friend who has spent many years in the Holy Land tells me that many of the sheepfolds near Bethlehem are in caves or under overhanging rocks. After the flock has grazed in the pasture all day, the shepherd herds the sheep to the side of a hill where such a formation affords shelter from the elements. Shepherds can sometimes be seen standing at the door of such a cave with their legs spread apart. One by one, the sheep come to the shepherd, who takes the head of each sheep into his hands and gently feels about the face for any scratches or wounds. He applies balm as needed and wipes the dirt and grime from the eyes. Then as the sheep walks through the shepherd's legs into the shelter of the cave, the shepherd runs his fingers through the sheep's wool, careful to find and remove any briars or thorns that may be caught there. Nursed, cleansed, caressed, and assured of the shepherd's love, the sheep enter the cave for the night and drop off to sleep.

Jesus calls himself the door of the sheep (John 10:7, 9). It is possible that he had in mind a scene such as the one I have just described. As the sheep pass through the legs of the shepherd to the security of the sheepfold, we must pass through Jesus into everlasting life, pausing to allow him to explore every corner of our being, healing our hurts and removing the grime from our hearts.

What is "everlasting life"? The answer is simpler than we often make it: "This is eternal life, that they know thee the only true God, and Jesus Christ whom thou has sent" (John 17:3). To know God through Jesus Christ *is* eternal life. It is a present reality, not merely for after we die, but for today as well. We begin to experience eternal life when we begin to know and trust Jesus. Then we find that eternal life *is* to know and trust Jesus. He is both the door and the destination.

MONDAY IN EASTER WEEK

The Paschal Feast

Grant, we pray, Almighty God, that we who celebrate with awe the Paschal feast may be found worthy to attain to everlasting joys.

Referring to Easter as the Paschal feast points to its connection with Passover. That connection may not be immediately apparent to many Christians, but it runs deep. Jesus' death and resurrection occurred during Passover week. Jesus is called the Lamb of God, a reference to the Passover sacrifice. Both Passover and Easter were rescue operations in which God broke the chains that had held his people captive. Both were at once political and spiritual events, bringing life out of death. The rituals commemorating those events, the Passover supper and the Christian Eucharist, are both symbolic meals uniting the people of God. Easter can be seen as the final chapter in the Passover story.

From our vantage point, Passover and Easter are one-of-a-kind events. But perhaps they are examples of what God is always and everywhere doing, the only difference being that in Passover and Easter, God has given us a glimpse of what he is about. Perhaps Passover and Easter are like snapshots of God, to be looked at, remembered, talked about, and celebrated later, but not unlike an eternity of other moments of which we are unaware. Perhaps the uniqueness of these two events is not that God has acted there, but that we have perceived God acting there.

I recall struggling as a child with mathematics. One evening I shall never forget. A particularly thorny problem had frustrated me for hours. I had written and erased so many times that my paper had become dirty and frayed. Finally I rubbed a hole in it. I was angry and afraid I would get a poor grade on the assignment. Then when the solution seemed hopelessly beyond me, it seemed to leap out from the page at me, and everything was instantly clear. I felt an exaltation rarely known since and that I can relive even now, decades later.

The solution was, of course, there all along. The obstruction was in my mind. When the obstruction was removed, I saw the truth for the first time. What had been a kind of unseen presence as I struggled with the problem suddenly became visible to me. When something of this sort happens, the solution to the problem is seen to apply to other problems as well. Eventually, a student's whole understanding of mathematics is enlarged.

Passover and Easter are like the solution to the mathematics problem. They provide us with a glimpse of God that informs other occasions in our lives and enables us to perceive the hand of God where we had seen only random events before. We see that as God broke the chains binding the Israelites in Egypt and Jesus in the tomb, he breaks the chains that bind us. Their stories become our own: we walk with the Israelites through the wilderness toward the promised land; we die and are raised with Christ.

Could Passover and Easter be uniquely revealing to us rather than unique in themselves? Might they appear commonplace from the other side of eternity? The answer to that question does not matter. It is sufficient for us that we have perceived God acting in Passover and Easter, and that seeing him in these redemptive moments has enabled us to see every moment as redemptive. That is why it is with awe that we celebrate the Paschal feast.

TUESDAY IN EASTER WEEK

Raised with Him

O God, who by the glorious resurrection of your Son Jesus Christ destroyed death and brought life and immortality to light: Grant that we, who have been raised with him, may abide in his presence and rejoice in the hope of eternal glory.

The great destroyer has been destroyed. God has destroyed death by the glorious resurrection of Jesus. We often fail to celebrate what God has done because we try to analyze, dissect, and explain it. How the resuscitation of a human body after three days could be possible, discrepancies among the canonical accounts of the empty tomb, where Jesus' soul went while he lay in the tomb, how quantum mechanics and relativity theory might shed light on the resurrection—these are interesting matters for speculation, but they divert our attention from *what* happened to *how* it happened. Such discussions are nonsense because the event itself is, in conventional thinking, nonsense. All the words and thoughts available to us fail to comprehend this victory. We come closest to it when we leave rational analysis behind and allow our imaginations to wander in poetry, song, fantasy, myth, art, drama, and dreams. Mystery and majesty are most at home there.

Resurrection becomes a reality for us when we experience the empty tomb in our own lives. We have been buried and raised with Christ, as St. Paul tells us (Romans 6:3–4). The cross, the grave, and the empty tomb are all experiences that we share with Christ—often through poetry, song, fantasy, myth, art, drama, and dreams. It is not a question of whether or how Jesus was raised from the dead. It is a question of where in our lives we experience the same power.

I was reflecting one day on the story of Lazarus, related in John 11. We know almost nothing about Lazarus, which invites us to put ourselves into the scene by filling in the details of his life with our own. I recalled a time when I had felt dead, when joy and faith were no more to me than vague memories of an earlier, almost forgotten day. I felt that Jesus had let me die. Reading the Lazarus story, I experienced his despair when, after Jesus had been summoned to the bedside of his critically ill friend, Jesus did not come. Jesus let Lazarus die, and only then did he come. Jesus wept as he stood at the mouth of the cave where Lazarus lay buried and bound in the burial shroud. In my mind I saw Jesus weeping for me. Within the tomb, I felt the darkness and the shroud around me—binding strips of pride, ambition, resentment, self-pity, and self-will. I smelled the odors of the tomb and felt the roaches and rats scurrying over me. I had begun to enjoy the tomb as I reflected on the injustice of it all; martyrdom became me, I told myself.

Then I heard the voice of Jesus from outside the tomb: *"Lazarus, come out!"* I rallied my rotting limbs, hurled myself off the stone slab onto the floor of the tomb, and lurched toward the sound of his voice. "I'm coming!" I tried to shout with what raspy voice I still could muster. Somehow I managed to reach the mouth of the cave. *"Unbind him; let him go,"* Jesus said. They did. It was the most terrifying thing anyone there had ever seen. I breathed the fresh air again.

When I experienced the Lazarus story as my own, I realized the resurrection is more than a strange story of something God did for Jesus two millennia ago. The resurrection is my story, a victory God has won for me, in the United States of America, two millennia later. It is also a victory he has won for his people in all times and in all places, and a victory that hints at the victory saints and angels celebrate in heaven.

George Herbert also experienced a time when he felt shriveled and dead, followed by an experience of resurrection:

> Who would have thought my shriveled heart
> Could have recovered greenness? It was gone
> Quite underground; as flowers depart
> To see their mother-root, when they have blown;
> Where they together
> All the hard weather,
> Dead to the world, keep house unknown.
>
> And now in age I bud again,
> After so many deaths I live and write;
> I once more smell the dew and rain,
> And relish versing: O my only light,
> It cannot be
> That I am he
> On whom thy tempests fell all night.

WEDNESDAY IN EASTER WEEK

Open the Eyes of Our Faith

O God, whose blessed Son made himself known to his disciples in the breaking of bread: Open the eyes of our faith, that we may behold him in all his redeeming work.

The interior of the New Cathedral in St. Louis, Missouri, is a stunning space, an enormous expanse of transepts and bays converging at the altar. The floor, ceiling, and walls of that vast room are covered with mosaics. Over forty million colored stones, most not more than an inch square, have been cemented onto the surfaces to form pictures of the great saints of the church, from apostolic times to the present Archdiocese of St. Louis. Standing in the cathedral and gazing at the surrounding surfaces, I feel myself surrounded by a great cloud of witnesses and want to break into some great hymn of the church triumphant such as "The church's one foundation" or "For all the saints."

But when I walk to the side of the room, stand within inches of one of the walls, and look at the stones and the masonry that holds them in place, the wall seems a mere hodge-podge of little colored rocks. From such close range, there is no apparent pattern to the stones, no sense of transcendent reality, just splotches of green or blue or gold rock stuck to a wall. One must turn around and look back toward the center to see that everything composes a glorious panorama of praise.

It is as if we live our entire lives not merely close to, but within one of the walls. I imagine the cathedral as the communion of saints and each baptized person as an individual stone among the millions of stones in the cathedral walls. My experience consists of relationships with a few other stones with which I am in direct contact. Through reading, conversation, and prayer, I may learn something of a few other stones elsewhere in the room. I hear rumors of purpose, order, and design, and I may believe what I hear. But I do not see it until I am given the power to gaze out from the spot where I live my life. Then I glimpse that great company of saints of which I am a tiny but essential part.

No one can fully understand the breadth and magnificence of what God is doing in his universe. We perceive only the events of our immediate neighborhood, which often seem ridiculous and mundane. There's old Mrs. Smith, with her jangling bracelets and her soupy piety. There's Mr. Jones who doesn't like children in church because they awaken him during the sermon. There's Miss

Jenkins, whose devotion to the Lord seems to consist chiefly in arranging flowers. There's Dr. Gonzalez who's always frowning and fidgeting and complaining about the budget. There's Mrs. Collins who sings every hymn too loud and a half tone flat. And there's the rector with his bumbling reading of the service and his arcane preaching. Can this be the communion of saints?

It is. But it is not the entire communion of saints. Each of these persons, like we ourselves, is a small stone, undistinguished when considered alone. Even a few stones together are undistinguished. But all partake of a reality that transcends them and of which they are only dimly aware.

It is because we often perceive even the people and events around us wrongly, failing to discern the glory and wisdom that is in them, that we pray that the eyes of our faith may be opened that we may behold Christ "in all his redeeming work." This requires us first to acknowledge our own limited vision, leading to a healthy humility and tolerance of others. When others seem undeserving, the likely explanation is that we are blind to the beauty in them that God sees and loves. When others differ from us in their perception of God, the likely explanation is that they perceive elements of God's creating and redeeming work that we cannot yet see. Each day is a potential new revelation, in response to which we might say, "I never suspected God would do *that*, in *that* way, through *that* person, for *that* end!"

Breaking of bread is a common, simple act. We break bread with people we acknowledge as equals, neither better nor worse than ourselves. Where differences of status are recognized, people do not eat together. When we break bread together at the Lord's table, everyone is an equal and all approach the table on the same terms: all hearts open, all desires known, no secrets hidden. The pretense that we are more deserving than the common, irritating, superficial people who approach the table alongside us is abandoned. We are all common, undistinguished little stones. But in the hands of God, we become part of a glorious work that transcends us.

THURSDAY IN EASTER WEEK

The New Covenant

*Almighty and everlasting God, who in the Paschal mystery
established the new covenant of reconciliation: Grant that all
who have been reborn into the fellowship of Christ's Body
may show forth in their lives what they profess by their faith.*

A covenant is an agreement or treaty between two parties that
structures the relationship between them. The Hebrew *berith*,
or covenant, was originally a political term, used for agreements
between nations or tribes, sometimes between equals but more
often between a major power and its vassals. The covenant was
initiated and its terms set by the stronger party.

The Bible contains several covenants between God and his
people, each initiated by God and its terms set by God. In every
case, the covenants are based on the love of God for his people.

What Christians call the "old covenant" was initiated by God
on Mount Sinai. It includes the Ten Commandments and other
laws designed to assure the chosen people that God loved them
and would protect them from danger. For their part, the people
promised, "All the words which the Lord has spoken we will do"
(Exodus 24:3).

But almost before those words were uttered, the people had
broken their promise. The old covenant therefore soon began to
revolve around the question, asked by God: *"What have you done?"*
The people replied by confessing their sins. A grieved God then
chastised his people and forgave them, for however unfaithful the

people might be, God is faithful. The people then sinned again, and God asked again: *"What have you done?"* The reply was the same, and God's response the same. Again and again, God caught his people behaving like disobedient children, heard their repentance, reprimanded them, and continued to love them.

The "new covenant" is the covenant established by Jesus Christ. It, too, is based on the love of God, and it revolves around the same question: "What have you done?" But now it is we who ask the question and God who answers: *"I have bound you to me forever. You can no longer drift away, however often you fail me, for with my blood I have soldered you to myself, and I shall be with you even in your disobedience. I have forgiven you. It is done. Nothing you do can undo it."*

FRIDAY IN EASTER WEEK

The Leaven of Malice and Wickedness

Almighty Father, who gave your only Son to die for our sins and to rise for our justification: Give us grace so to put away the leaven of malice and wickedness, that we may always serve you in pureness of living and truth.

The preamble to this prayer is the gospel story in a capsule: God is our almighty Father—creator, teacher, disciplinarian, guardian. When we turned from him, he gave his only Son to die on our behalf. In fulfilling his Father's will, the Son swept death aside, setting us right with God again. The petition and result clause of the collect speak of the changes in our lives that Christ's victory is intended to produce.

Leaven is a foreign agent, an impurity introduced into dough, causing the dough to rise. It is an infection, a defilement, doing its work silently and discreetly. Fermentation is a gradual corrupting, a progressive debasing of the entire lump of dough as the yeast rises and the dough is transformed. Given favorable conditions, the tiniest amount of leaven will spread and corrupt an entire loaf. It is like the first weed in a garden: if not uprooted, it will multiply until weeds strangle every other plant. It is like the first mold on a morsel of food: if not cut away, it will consume the whole.

The leaven of malice and wickedness often finds a home in our souls, robbing us of our freedom and our true identity. Even as we seek to celebrate the Easter victory, this leaven can be working within to corrupt and consume us.

Once many years ago, a woman in my parish whom I had trusted began spreading unfounded and damaging rumors about my personal life. The woman's position in the church gave her a wide audience. Even some who knew me well began to question my character. I came to see this woman as my enemy and grew obsessed by thoughts of what I'd like to do and say to her. Driving down the road, I rehearsed caustic speeches in my mind. I thought of little else. Finally I realized that while I could not control what this woman said, I could choose my response to her. My most dangerous enemy, I came to see, was not the woman, but the angry, bitter spirit within me. By consuming all my thoughts and energy, that spirit had immobilized me and choked my ability to serve and enjoy God. The leaven of malice and wickedness had taken root in me, multiplying like cancerous cells through my soul to corrupt and consume.

I decided to focus on my own transgressions rather than the woman's, upon putting my own spiritual house in order. I began to pray for the woman. At first these prayers stuck in my throat, but in time I came actually to desire for her what I prayed for—healing and joy. When that happened, I found healing and joy for myself as well.

To serve God "in pureness of living and truth" is to be freed from all that is foreign to our nature as God intends it. God intends that we serve and enjoy him. Whatever contaminates or pollutes our souls, blocking us from living obediently and contentedly at home with our Father, must be rooted out. Only then can we experience "the unleavened bread of sincerity and truth" (Corinthians 5:8).

SATURDAY IN EASTER WEEK

We Thank You

We thank you, heavenly Father, that you have delivered us from the dominion of sin and death and brought us into the kingdom of your Son; and we pray that, as by his death he has recalled us to life, so by his love he may raise us to eternal joys.

This is the only collect that thanks God for anything, perhaps because the collects are normally prayed within the context of worship services that contain other expressions of thanksgiving.

The prayer thanks God for the benefits given to us through his Son. It hinges on two synonyms, *dominion* and *kingdom*. Having begun in "the dominion of sin and death," we thank God for bringing us into "the kingdom of your Son."

Dominions and kingdoms are places where someone is in charge, and everyone knows it. Individual freedom, individual rights, individual choice—these are not highly valued in dominions and kingdoms. Order is the prevailing value. Everyone is assigned a place in the great scheme of things. One does not choose or create one's own place, and everyone is expected to accept the place assigned and to behave accordingly.

The notion of a dominion or kingdom sounds archaic to many modern ears. It is contrary to the democratic individualism that Americans hold dear. In an age when many Americans are shouting for less government and greater freedom to believe what they wish, spend their money as they wish, dispose of their property as they wish, educate their children as they wish, and do with their bodies as they wish, it seems incongruous that we should be thanking God for making us citizens of a dictatorship.

Many people, however—certainly many Americans—are subject to a dictator and do not know it. Millions are slaves to the dominion of sin and death, where the devil holds sway. That dominion is a prison. The chains that bind us in our cells are self-imposed at first. In the beginning, we have choices: we choose to view ourselves as economic beings, to produce and consume, to exhaust ourselves seeking success, to ingest addictive substances, to break sacred promises, to postpone the intimate relationships and quiet times that might nurture the soul.

Before long, however, we have no more choices. Our habits have been formed and we are no longer conscious of any other way to live. We cannot choose something we don't know is there, and when we surround ourselves with self-will, we see nothing but self-will, and we choose what we see. The dominion of sin and death comes to seem normal. We are miserable and do not know it, like the characters in C. S. Lewis's *The Great Divorce*, who are so consumed with self-will that they do not realize they live in hell and decline to reside in heaven when they are invited to relocate there.

It is from this dominion that Jesus Christ has delivered us. The kingdom of Christ is like all other kingdoms and dominions, including that of sin and death, in one respect: someone is in charge and everyone knows it. But everything depends on who that someone is. Where Christ is in charge, there is no compulsive, self-willed behavior. He is in charge because he has been invited to be in charge; we are his subjects because we choose to obey him. Our ruler knows and loves his subjects, gives himself for his subjects. He sets the captive soul free, first by loving us, then by rooting out the stagnant evil of the past, and finally by making our souls his home.

We are still subject to a power from outside ourselves, but now the power is Christ, "whose service is perfect freedom," as the Book of Common Prayer (p. 57) says. We are free because Christ enables us to become the creatures we were intended to be. The transformation is gradual, sometimes imperceptible, but bit by bit, day by day, the chains are loosened and the sinews of our souls begin to stretch and grow. Freedom is Christ's gift; thankfulness is our response.

SECOND SUNDAY OF EASTER
(See Thursday in Easter Week)

THIRD SUNDAY OF EASTER
(See Wednesday in Easter Week)

FOURTH SUNDAY OF EASTER
The Good Shepherd

O God, whose son Jesus is the good shepherd of your people: Grant that when we hear his voice we may know him who calls us each by name, and follow where he leads.

I listen for your voice, Jesus, but I cannot distinguish it among all the other sounds. Cars honk in the streets, airplanes roar overhead, cash registers jingle, televisions bark empty messages, even air conditioners and refrigerators hum and block out the voice I would hear. I must learn to be quiet within, even when noises surround me on the outside. This will take more than a few quick moments between phone calls. It will require me to go deep into the cellar of my soul where noise does not penetrate and to remain there until I hear the sound of your voice.

I can hear you now, my Shepherd. *"Taste the water,"* you say. Before me is a pool of clear, still water. I bend down and drink. I was thirsty and did not know it. I gulp swallow after swallow. Finally, my thirst is slaked. Then I plunge into the pool and let the cool water envelop me. My hot, achy joints are rejuvenated; I am refreshed through and through. When I look up, I see you standing on the bank, laughing. It is the laughter of a parent watching a child play for the first time in the surf.

"This moment is my gift to you, but you are not to remain here. I must lead you on from here. You cannot avoid the valley of the shadow of death. I have not promised to lead you through green pastures and beside still waters only. You must choose: seek comfortable places and follow whatever shepherd promises to lead you there, or seek me and follow where I lead. Seeking comfortable places does not guarantee that you will find them, for many shepherds promise what they cannot deliver. But seeking me guarantees that you will find me, for you will discover that you are not the seeker, as you suppose, but the sought. It is I who find you, not you who find me. The green pastures and the dark valleys are both holy places when you allow me to find you there and when you follow me.

"Do not be afraid. I will discipline you with my rod and staff. You will not always enjoy this discipline, but my rod and staff will pull you away from the dangers of foolishness and self-will. I will lead you through green pastures and dark valleys. I will anoint you with oil to heal your wounds. When you grow weary, I will take you to rest in the sheepfold."

You are the good Shepherd, Jesus, the delectable Shepherd.

I want to be near you, to see the black earth ground into your clothes, smell you as you hold me in your arms, feel the moisture of your sweat, your ribs pressing against mine, your stubble beard against my cheek. I want to hear you breathing, panting, humming, whispering.

"Richard?"

Did you call me? Did you call my name?

"I called your name because I love you. Just as you enjoy pressing against me, smelling me, and hearing me breathing next to you, so do I enjoy you. I call you by name not because I love humanity or the world or the cosmos (although I do love those things), but because I love you. I love your mussy hair, your sore feet, the sound of your voice, your forgetful mind, your winsome humor, your dreams and imaginings and fantasies, all that you are and will be and could ever be. I love the way you look, sound, smell, taste, think, and feel. Nothing you can say or think or do will change my mind about you. I call your name because I love you, Richard."

FIFTH SUNDAY OF EASTER

Everlasting Life

Almighty God, whom truly to know is everlasting life: Grant us so perfectly to know your Son Jesus Christ to be the way, the truth, and the life, that we may steadfastly follow his steps in the way that leads to eternal life.

A s a child, when I heard the preacher speak of everlasting or eternal life, I envisioned an endless sequence of years, a continuation of time as we know it, but with improved conditions: no sickness, no arguing, lots of fun things to do.

At some point, I realized this was naive. I then began to visualize time as a yardstick on the floor, with my life on earth taking place somewhere on that thirty-six-inch line—say, for example, between the seventeenth- and eighteenth-inch markings. I have some knowledge of the seventeen inches of history that lie behind me, but none of what lies ahead of me. I don't even know whether I live at inch three or inch thirty-three. God, I thought, stands above the yardstick and looks down at all thirty-six inches at once. He sees past, present, and future in a single glance—everything is present to God. Everlasting life would be the ability to see things as God sees them, something I might look forward to after I die.

There may be more truth to this picture of everlasting life than to my earlier one, but something important is still missing. One day I was reflecting on the first few verses of John 14, in which Jesus tells the disciples, "In my Father's house are many rooms." I had always liked that passage because I had envisioned myself in heaven, sitting in the room I hoped would be prepared for me: a library with bookcases lining the walls and current periodicals on the table, comfortable chairs, a sound system playing Mozart in the background, and a picture window overlooking a garden tended by someone else. As I was enjoying this picture in my mind, a voice seemed to say to me: *"What makes you think I'd prepare the same room for you that you'd prepare for yourself?"* That was a jarring thought. Then the voice said: *"The many rooms are all for you. You will move from one room to another."* I realized I had thought of everlasting life as a static thing, a condition to be arrived at and then enjoyed in perpetuity. But perhaps everlasting life is a flowing, evolving thing, a continuation of the growth that begins in this life. I recalled the line from the Episcopal burial office in which we pray that the deceased "may go from strength to strength in the life of perfect service in thy heavenly kingdom" (Book of Common Prayer, p. 481). St. Paul spoke of the same thing when he wrote of our "being changed . . . from one degree of glory to another" (2 Corinthians 3:18), and several of the great saints have written of the next life as a continual journey.

This new vision of everlasting life as moving from room to room, from strength to strength, from glory to glory, felt like a revelation to me. But still, something was missing. Besides growing and moving, just what is everlasting or eternal life? The Gospel of John tells us that eternal life is to know God and Jesus Christ whom God has sent (17:3). I began to understand the knowledge of God not as information to be acquired, like the price of a pork chop or the shortest route to Chillicothe, but as an ever-deepening relationship. As the love, power, and wisdom of God are infinite, our knowledge of God can never be complete, not in this life and not in the next life. Our knowledge of the Lord grows ever more intimate and more profound. Each room in our Father's house contains a fresh revelation of his glory.

Sixth Sunday of Easter

Good Things as Surpass Our Understanding

O God, you have prepared for those who love you such good things as surpass our understanding: Pour into our hearts such love towards you, that we, loving you in all things and above all things, may obtain your promises, which exceed all that we can desire.

We instinctively love what we can understand and control. When I was a young man and realized I did not know the answers to all of life's perplexing questions, I undertook to find the answers. Then I would convince people of them. I would do this through the force of my hard work and intelligence. I would be in control. If I came across something beyond my understanding, I would investigate it until I did understand it. The notion that some things might be by nature beyond my understanding did not then occur to me.

Only later did I conclude that ignorance is not something to be overcome, but my natural condition, as much a part of me as gender or skin color. I could like it or not like it, but I wasn't going to change it. I decided to accept my ignorance and learn how an ignoramus goes about loving, serving, and enjoying his God.

Letting go of my desire to understand and control did not come easily or quickly. I had long fancied myself an empty vessel to be filled, and only gradually did I begin to relinquish the desire to fill that vessel myself with the knowledge I would acquire. I am still relinquishing that desire. The more I submit my emptiness to God and let him fill me, the more God gives me "such good things as surpass our understanding."

As God pours his love more deeply into me, I am beginning to see God present "in all things and above all things." I hear him saying to me, "*Look for me everywhere. I will teach you to love me in laughter and in tears, in thrills and in boredom, in pleasure and in pain, in certainty and in doubt, in company and alone, in victory and in defeat, in good and in evil, in yourself and in others, in friend and in foe, in life and in death. Your thoughts and feelings are like the tide, coming and going, rising and falling, in and out. You often forget me, but I will teach you to love me in all things, even in your forgetfulness.*

"*I will also teach you to love me above all things. Though you see me in all things, I remain beyond what you can see, and you must never think that because you have loved me in what you see that you have loved me entirely. Love me patiently, always anticipating the new love I will pour into you when I have further prepared you.*"

And then, Lord, will I obtain your promises that exceed all that I can desire?

"You will already have obtained my promises. When you have fully surrendered your desire to know and control and have learned to love me in all things and above all things, you will have received my promises. What you formerly desired will be exceeded by what is already yours."

· ❧ ·

ASCENSION DAY

That He Might Fill All Things

Almighty God, whose blessed Son our Savior Jesus Christ ascended far above all heavens that he might fill all things: Mercifully give us faith to perceive that, according to his promise, he abides with his Church on earth, even to the end of the ages.

St. Luke gives us two accounts of Christ's ascension into heaven. The first comes at the very end of his Gospel and makes no mention of clouds or of the disciples' gazing into heaven. Those details come in Luke's second account, in the first chapter of the Acts of the Apostles. They have been the cause of some derision on the part of scoffers because they seem crass and unbelievable: "Was Jesus in a hot-air balloon? Or did a tornado take him away, the way Dorothy was taken out of Kansas?" These details have embarrassed believers and given nonbelievers an occasion to poke fun at religious belief. During the middle part of the twentieth century, theologians labored to "demythologize" the Christian message and to eliminate the Bible's spatial imagery of heaven and earth, descending and ascending, up and down.

One doesn't hear much of that sort of thing today. That is partly because any other language would entail other, equally problematic images. C. S. Lewis saw this even as demythologizing was coming into vogue. He wrote in 1944: "To say that God 'enters' the natural order involves just as much spatial imagery as to say that He 'comes down'; one has simply substituted horizontal (or undefined) for vertical movement. To say that He is 're-absorbed' into the Noumenal is better than to say He 'ascended' into Heaven, only if the picture of something dissolving in warm fluid, or being sucked into a throat, is less misleading than the picture of a bird, or a balloon, going up. All language, except about objects of sense, is metaphorical through and through" (*God in the Dock*, p. 71).

We could do worse than to bind ourselves to a literal view of the ascension, but we need not accept a literal view. Ascending is a common metaphor for success and joy: students "go up" to the next grade; a good worker is promoted to a "higher" position; a happy memory is a "high point" in our lives. To what success or joy, then, does the story of Christ's ascension into heaven point?

The prayer alludes to it by a clause from Ephesians 4:10, "that he might fill all things." This means there is no person, place, or time left unvisited by Christ. We are forever trying to limit Christ's domain by separating people and things into two categories, those brought under his rule and those still outside it. The ascension proclaims that the second category does not exist: Christ's reign encompasses all. He binds earth and heaven in himself. The distinction between the sacred and the profane has been erased: all is sacred.

If we are to speak of such things at all, it is best to do so in fanciful images, like those of dreams, myths, and science fiction novels. Rising into the clouds is as good an image as any. To call these images fanciful does not mean that they are not true, but that their truth is suggestive and elusive, not to be pinned down by rational analysis. Howard Chandler Robbins wrote of such truth in obviously fanciful language:

And have the bright immensities received our risen Lord,
where light-years frame the Pleiades and point Orion's sword?
Do flaming suns His footsteps trace through corridors sublime,
the Lord of interstellar space and Conqueror of time?
(*Hymnal 1982*, #459)

It is permissible, perhaps advisable, not to speak of such things
at all. Words define and limit. Richard Hooker, that wise and
gracious man, knew that silence is often the most eloquent testimony. He was writing about the theological enterprise in general,
but he could have had the ascension specifically in mind when he
composed the opening chapter of his great theological work four
centuries ago: "Dangerous it were for the feeble brain of man to
wade far into the doings of the Most High; whom although to
know be life, and joy to make mention of his name; yet our sound-
est knowledge is to know that we know him not as indeed he is,
neither can know him: and our safest eloquence concerning him is
our silence, when we confess without confession that his glory is
inexplicable, his greatness above our capacity and reach. He is
above, and we upon earth; therefore it behoveth our words to be
wary and few" (*Of the Laws of Ecclesiastical Polity*, I, i, 2).

With Him Continually Dwell

*Grant, we pray, Almighty God, that as we believe your only-
begotten Son our Lord Jesus Christ to have ascended into
heaven, so we may also in heart and mind there ascend, and
with him continually dwell.*

Separation from those we love is usually a sad event. Yet the disciples felt "great joy" after Jesus departed from them (Luke 24:52). Morton Kelsey feels this is the strangest feature of Luke's account of the ascension. He writes that had he been making up the story himself, he would have probably written: "And leaving the mount of Olivet with their eyes running with tears they said to one another, 'It was a wonderful experience while it lasted. It will be lonely as we await his return. So sad, so strange the days that are no more.' Then they went back with heavy hearts and grim determination to the tasks Jesus had appointed them to do" (*Resurrection*, p. 136).

But there is joy, not sadness, when the risen Christ ascends to heaven. This is apparently because the New Testament authors and early church fathers soon moved beyond the sense of Christ's absence. There are references to Christ's continuing presence among the faithful. There are also, paradoxically, references to Christ's having ascended into the sky. But there is no mention of his *absence*.

The key to solving this puzzle lies in a suggestive image found in the Epistle to the Hebrews. Much of that epistle's message is difficult for modern readers because it is couched in ancient concepts no longer widely understood. Hebrews offers one image, however, that is as readily grasped today as it was in the first century: Christ as the "pioneer" of our salvation, the "forerunner on our behalf," the "pioneer and perfecter of our faith" (Hebrews 2:10; 6:20; 12:2).

Imagine yourself lost in a dense forest, surrounded by wild animals and hidden dangers. You are wandering through thorny thickets. You stumble and bruise your knees. You're hungry, thirsty, and exhausted. You feel helpless and frightened. Suddenly you come upon a path. Someone has traveled this way before and cleared the brush, cut through the briars, and left markers indicating the way to safety. This someone has even chained the dangerous beasts who inhabit the forest and built guardrails along the roadside so that you may travel without fear. This someone has also left food and drink for you along the way. You meet other travelers who tell you something of the pioneer or forerunner who did all this; in preparing this way for you to follow, he endured many dangers, deprivations, and degradations.

Wherever we go, whatever we experience, Christ has preceded us and prepared the way. All ground is holy ground because he has been there. This prayer refers to our ascending to heaven "in heart and mind" in order that we may continually dwell with Christ. An event of the heart and mind is an event that engages our imaginations. We fully take part in it when we release our imaginations to soar and roam wherever God will lead them. It is not too fanciful, I think, to imagine ourselves far beyond this time and place, in an intergalactic procession, traveling through the light-years among the stars. We follow in the train of Jesus, sailing safely along the way he has gone before. We do not know where he is leading us, but we know Jesus, and we follow because we trust him and because the darkness will descend if we dally. Finally, we arrive at his Father's house. Jesus enters and we overhear a conversation from within:

"Welcome home, Son! And who are these others with you?"
"They're my friends, every one of them."
"Then bring them in, and let the feasting begin!"

SEVENTH SUNDAY OF EASTER: THE SUNDAY AFTER ASCENSION DAY

Do Not Leave Us Comfortless

O God, the King of glory, you have exalted your only Son Jesus Christ with great triumph to your kingdom in heaven: Do not leave us comfortless, but send us your Holy Spirit to strengthen us, and exalt us to that place where our Savior Christ has gone before.

This prayer is based on an ancient Christian antiphon sung at Vespers on Ascension Day. The antiphon says, "O Lord, King of glory, Lord of hosts, who today did ascend in triumph above the heavens, leave us not orphans, but send upon us the promise of the Father, even the Spirit of Truth." The antiphon echoes John 14:18 (KJV): "I will not leave you orphans; I will come to you." In composing this collect for the 1549 Book of Common Prayer, Archbishop Cranmer deleted the reference to orphans, substituting the weaker and more generalized wording, "leave us not comfortless," which is retained in the present version.

The image of the orphan is a vivid one that suggests the anxiety behind the words, "Do not leave us comfortless." Mature children are eager to establish themselves as independent, self-sufficient adults. Loving parents, recognizing this as a good and normal thing, do not hold onto them. This process can be painful both to children and to parents. I remember the college graduation of our three sons, officiating at their weddings, and watching them relocate to distant cities and undertake careers. I was happy for them, but my happiness was tinged with something resembling grief. I wanted to hold onto my children, but I knew I must resist that temptation. I would not leave them comfortless, but it had to be a comfort different from the comfort I had given when they were younger.

My own move toward maturity was frightening and demoralizing. After graduating from college, I moved to a city where I knew no one and began to look for work. My parents were 250 miles away. I took a small basement apartment near the local university and began responding to "Help wanted" ads in the newspaper. At first, my new independence exhilarated me. I had saved enough money to live for a few weeks on my own. After interviewing for jobs during the day, I spent my evenings reading and listening to music. For the first time, I bought my own groceries and ate what I wanted, when I wanted it. My life was my own. I was "free" as never before.

My exhilaration was short-lived. Several possible employers declined to hire me, for reasons they did not explain. My savings dwindled. Fear began to gnaw at my heart. The pleasure of evenings spent reading and listening to music quickly gave way to a raw loneliness. One morning, still without work and desperate to hear the voice of someone who knew and cared for me, I telephoned my father. We talked for only a few minutes. I don't recall what I said, but five hours later, a knock came at my apartment door. My father had taken off from his job to come to me. Never in my life was I so happy to see him, and never had I been so certain of his love for me.

My father demonstrated his continuing love for me by coming to me when I had grown weary and despondent, but he did not stay with me and he did not suggest that I return home to live once again under his roof. My future could not be a return to the past. But my future would grow from the past as a tree grows from a sapling. Although I would never again live in the town where I had grown up and where my parents continued to reside, I would, in my own way and place, live the life they had helped me prepare for. I would make my own way, but the spirit and values of those who had come before would guide and strengthen me. I would not be an orphan; I would not be comfortless.

After Jesus ascended into heaven, the disciples were on their own for the first time. We are told they "devoted themselves to prayer" (Acts 1:14). This prayer may have contained some excitement at first, but surely the excitement soon gave way to confusion and fear. What were the disciples to do now? Where could they turn? Who would strengthen and care for them? The collect for the Sunday after Ascension Day therefore has a plaintive tone: the one who guided and strengthened us has gone. Do not leave us as orphans, alone, comfortless, but send us someone to strengthen us that we may come to the place where we feel both free and secure.

The disciples had to grow up, both for their own sakes and for the future of the church. This would not have happened if Jesus had remained with them. They had to learn to take the initiative, to struggle with life's ambiguities, to make their own decisions and live with the results of those decisions. They would discover as they grew up that although Jesus was no longer physically with them, they remained part of Jesus and could still depend upon his power, guidance, and love. But no longer as children.

THE DAY OF PENTECOST: WHITSUNDAY

The Preaching of the Gospel

Almighty God, on this day you opened the way of eternal life to every race and nation by the promised gift of your Holy Spirit: Shed abroad this gift throughout the world by the preaching of the Gospel, that it may reach to the ends of the earth.

The story of the disciples preaching the gospel in every known tongue on the Jewish Feast of Pentecost in Acts 2 suggests the opening affirmation of this prayer, saying that on this day God opened the way to eternal life to every race and nation. Pentecost also suggests St. John the Divine's vision of a great multitude in heaven "which no man could number, from every nation, from all tribes and people and tongues" (Revelation 7:9).

In keeping with the Pentecost account in Acts, the prayer names preaching as the primary means by which the gospel is to be spread to the ends of the earth—and preaching is the church's responsibility. If God has opened the way of eternal life to all, it seems he has entrusted the task of issuing the invitation to a third party, the church.

Preaching is an important undertaking, for two reasons. First, preaching brings those who do not know the love of God to accept and rejoice in it. Preaching takes different forms. In the first century, when the New Testament was written, preaching was normally a communicating of the gospel story to persons who had never heard it, often done in synagogues and in public places. The gospel is still preached primarily to nonbelievers in many parts of the world. Elsewhere, however, preaching is a communicating of the gospel to those who have heard it many times, or at least heard of it. Often what they have heard is a warped version of the story, more bad news than good, something that they have rightly rejected. In such cases, effective preaching must wipe clean the soiled slate; the injurious work of the past must be undone before the gospel can be heard.

Many people think of preaching as a formalized activity of priests and ministers, usually done from a pulpit on Sunday mornings in the context of a worship service. This is often a harmless undertaking, sometimes even helpful, but sermons have the reputation of being dull, and to say that someone is "preachy" is not to pay a compliment. In my experience, even good sermons rarely bring people to Christ. I believe this to be true even in churches where the preacher regularly issues an altar call, inviting members of the congregation to step forward and give their lives to Christ. Those who come forward do so for a variety of reasons, some having little to do with Christian commitment. The positive impact of good sermons is probably like that of drops of water falling onto a crusty, dry sponge: the first few drops have little effect, but many drops over time will soften and saturate the sponge. Good sermons are like that, cumulative in their effect. Unfortunately, bad sermons work the same way.

The most effective preaching is not done from the pulpit or on Sunday morning. It is done in hospitals, restaurants, automobiles, offices, classrooms, bedrooms—wherever Christians live out their discipleship. Sometimes the best preaching is done by means other than words. Simple acts of selfless love say more about God than volumes of verbal testimony. As C. S. Lewis has commented, the good news is often spread by a kind of infection, one person "catching it" from another.

The second reason preaching is important is that it is one of the means by which God invites his church to serve as his agent, to take part in his work, to bring all the world to eternal life. God invites us to become his colleagues, his fellow-workers, his friends. When the church fails to preach the gospel, we lose the opportunity to work alongside God and to share his joy.

Too often we imagine that God must rely on us to do his work for him. We act as if our sermons, programs, committees, and campaigns are essential to spreading the gospel. God grants us the privilege of sharing his work of redemption not because he requires our expertise and eloquence, but for the joy we receive in sharing in God's work. Our activities can be the means God uses to open the way of eternal life, but they are always means, never ends, and God does not depend upon them. When we begin to act as if what we do is essential, then God cannot work through us and will find other means. Sometimes I think the best thing the church could do is to discontinue some of our activities, and then get out of God's way. That might even be a sermon.

THE LIGHT OF YOUR HOLY SPIRIT

O God, who on this day taught the hearts of your faithful people by sending to them the light of your Holy Spirit: Grant us by the same Spirit to have a right judgment in all things, and evermore to rejoice in his holy comfort.

This prayer begins by recalling a past event, then asks that the same thing, or something like it, be granted to us today. The past event, recounted in Acts 2, is one of the most perplexing phenomena to occur in the history of the early church, the gift of the Holy Spirit on the Jewish feast of Pentecost, fifty days after Easter.

What happened at Pentecost? The disciples were changed. Still stunned by the crucifixion, the empty tomb, and the ascension, they had done little more than cast lots to select a successor to Judas Iscariot. But what were the disciples to do, and where would they find the strength and wisdom to do it? As the disciples gathered at a home in Jerusalem to observe the feast of Pentecost, the sound of a mighty wind filled the house, tongues of fire appeared over the disciples' heads, and they began to speak in strange languages. The noise attracted a crowd. Everyone was bewildered, some suspecting the disciples were drunk.

Then Peter began to speak as he had never spoken before. Having denied that he knew Jesus less than two months earlier, then befuddled and remorseful, Peter suddenly spoke with compelling authority. He quoted the Jewish scriptures. He announced that Jesus had risen from the dead. He asserted that he and the other disciples were witnesses to this fact. "Let all the house of Israel therefore know assuredly that God has made him both Lord and Christ, this Jesus whom you crucified" (Acts 2:36) he said. It was the first of countless speeches, often followed by persecution and martyrdom, by the disciples and those who would come after them, in every language and in every corner of the globe. It was the birthday of the Christian church.

Led by Peter, at Pentecost the disciples received clarity of mind, strength of will, and a power from beyond themselves. God taught their hearts by sending the light of the Holy Spirit, as the collect says. The Holy Spirit still gives this gift to those who ask for it.

The first thing is to ask, as this prayer does. Often we must ask for what we need without knowing what that is. The disciples did not know to ask for the gifts they received on that first Christian Pentecost, and we often cannot know what we need. Years ago, I found myself in a job where I felt I was suffocating spiritually. I prayed for guidance. Should I remain in that position despite my discomfort? Should I resign? Should I change careers? I begged God for clarity and direction. What I received was something very different, the ability to laugh at myself and my discomfort. It was as if God said to me, *"Quit your caterwauling. If you say you trust me, then trust me. For now, get on about your business. I'll take care of it when I'm ready."* I did, and God did. I believe that was a gift of the Holy Spirit.

The gifts of the Holy Spirit are rarely, perhaps never, merely gifts for individual Christians. The disciples may have felt edified, comforted, or strengthened by the Pentecost experience, but that was not its purpose. The outpouring of the Holy Spirit on that first Christian Pentecost was the beginning of the expansion of the Christian church to all peoples. Looking back on my own experience of praying for guidance when I was in discomfort in my job, I see that receiving the gift of the Holy Spirit served to prepare me for work I was later to do, where the ability to laugh at myself would be important. I was grateful that I also felt comforted by the experience; but God's primary purpose, I believe, was not to comfort me, but to strengthen and prepare me for the work of building up his church in another place, at another time.

Sometimes we do not want the gift given. It is easy to pray for an outpouring of the Holy Spirit, but will we like or accept the outpouring that is given? I was once rector of a parish where a small and deeply committed group of parishioners had kept the congregation alive during a time of internal controversy and declining membership. They prayed faithfully and often for the health of their church. Then suddenly, the membership more than doubled in a short period. The leadership patterns and dynamics of parish life were radically altered. A new church had to be constructed to accommodate all the people. Although nearly everyone was pleased that the parish was growing, the side effects of this growth were painful for some. Each person came to terms with the new situation in his or her own way; a few left the parish. The key for us all was to allow Christ to align our hearts, minds, and wills with his own and thereby to accept what the Holy Spirit was doing among us. Each had to say, with Christ in the garden, "Not my will, but thine be done" (Luke 22:42). The result of such faithfulness is often surprising.

The Sundays after Pentecost

FIRST SUNDAY AFTER PENTECOST: TRINITY SUNDAY

The Glory of the Eternal Trinity

Almighty and everlasting God, you have given to us your ser-vants grace, by the confession of a true faith, to acknowledge the glory of the eternal Trinity, and in the power of your divine Majesty to worship the Unity: Keep us steadfast in this faith and worship, and bring us at last to see you in your one and eternal glory.

The classical exposition of the doctrine of the Trinity in the Western church is contained in a seldom read document called the Athanasian Creed, found on page 864 of the Book of Common Prayer. I know of no one who, having read the Athanasian Creed, has been moved to shout "Eureka!" For sheer theological density, it has been rarely rivaled and never surpassed. One of its lines reads, "The Father incomprehensible, the Son incomprehensible, the Holy Ghost incomprehensible," to which someone once retorted, "The whole damned thing incomprehensible."

It's tempting to dismiss the Trinity as a harmless and irrelevant pastime for the intellectually precocious, "something put in by theologians to make it more difficult—nothing to do with daily life or ethics," as Dorothy Sayers commented in her book *Creed or Chaos.*

Part of the problem arises from our tendency to confuse the doctrine of the Trinity with reality. The Trinity points to something both real and important, but is itself a construct of the human

mind. It is like a map. The symbols on a map are merely represen-
tations of human thoughts, but a wise traveler pays attention to
them because they are based on realities encountered by earlier
travelers. So, too, the doctrine of the Trinity is a product of the
human mind, but it is the result of Christians reflecting upon real
experiences of God. It can help steer us clear of the treacherous
swamps of fanaticism and error.

Imagine a fish swimming in an aquarium. The fish knows
nothing of the maker of the aquarium or the person who purifies
the water and drops food into the aquarium each day. This is
because the fish's understanding is limited. The aquarium is part of
the decor of a room, designed to satisfy the artistic taste of a man
or woman, but the fish knows nothing of rooms, art, men, or
women. Human nature is beyond a fish's understanding.

Our ignorance of God is of the same sort. Human experience is
limited by the confines of the physical universe and the brief dura-
tion of human life. Of what larger reality these phenomena are a
part, we cannot know. Certainly our minds cannot comprehend it.
Still less can we comprehend the One who designs and creates it.

Human beings are not fish. So far as we know, fish possess no
inkling of a reality beyond themselves nor a longing to experience
it. Human beings, however, experience inklings and longings for
God. It is as if the fish were to brush against the aquarium's glass
walls and know that something must lie beyond them. We know
our world is a good place, generously endowed with everything we
need, but we also suspect that there is something more, and we
groan for it.

The suspicion that there is more derives from the events of our
lives and our reflection upon them. Many of these events are acts
of what we call "grace," unearned goodness. Some recur from day
to day—sunlight, nourishment, work to challenge us, the goodwill
of friends and family. Others are unique and occur but once—
flashes of insight, recovery from illness, unexpected gifts and
pleasures. We have a sense that these acts of grace come to us from
an unseen Giver.

Reflecting upon these events and the knowledge we derive

from them leads us to strange surmises about the nature of that Giver. Perhaps the strangest of these surmises is the doctrine of the Trinity. It is strange because it is entirely incomprehensible. This should not surprise us, for if a fish were able to reflect on its experiences in the aquarium and postulate what sort of being a man might be, its postulations would sound like nonsense to other fish. But such postulations would not be false on that account. Incomprehensibility may result from the limited perspective of the thinker rather than from the senselessness of the thought.

We experience ourselves as created and sustained. For that reason, we speak of God the Father. We experience ourselves as befriended and redeemed by Jesus. For that reason, we speak of God the Son. We experience ourselves as made holy and renewed within. For that reason, we speak of God the Spirit. Moreover, we believe that these experiences of God point, however faintly, to something more than our experience, to the nature of God himself. God is *relationship*, moving, giving, loving. And so arises talk of the Trinity and the Unity, three in one and one in three—"The Father incomprehensible, the Son incomprehensible, and the Holy Ghost incomprehensible"—yet not three incomprehensibles but one incomprehensible.

We do well to acknowledge the incomprehensibility of God and then stop trying to comprehend. The lust for comprehension arises from our idolatrous desire to see as God sees, to be as God is. When we fancy that we have done this, we magnify our meager ideas into absolute truths and refuse to tolerate those with other ideas, much less learn from them. The better stance is one of humility, adoration, and gratitude. Christians experience a God who creates, redeems, and sanctifies. The doctrine of the Trinity is the response of the mind; humility, adoration, and gratitude are the responses of the heart and will.

Shall we ever transcend the confines of our minds and gaze directly upon God in his one and eternal glory? God is fashioning us for that fuller vision. As it is granted, we shall likely still fail to comprehend. But our humility, adoration, and gratitude will have cause to abound all the more.

. ❧ .

PROPER 1

What You Have Wrought in Us

Remember, O Lord, what you have wrought in us and not what we deserve; and, as you have called us to your service, make us worthy of our calling.

All ages are present in my soul, and all kingdoms, and God blessed forever. And thus Jesus Christ is seen in me, and dwelleth in me, when I believe upon him. And thus all saints are in me, and I in them. And thus all angels and the eternity and infinity of God are in me for evermore, I being the living temple and comprehensor of them. (Thomas Traherne, *Centuries of Meditations*, I, 100)

All things are dusted with glory because God has imagined them and called them into being. Glory winks at glory from subatomic particles to outstretched galactic clusters; from fire and heat, winter and summer, dews and frosts; from mountains, valleys, plains, rivers, seas, deserts, swamps, jungles, meadows, tundras. And from every living thing, including you. God has wrought his glory in you. Every creature is present in you and you in every creature because the glory of God glistens in all that God creates.

God himself glistens in us, as a composer sings in his song. But when a song is written and finished, it assumes an existence apart from its creator. Nothing God creates ever exists apart from him. The glory with which creation shines is a living, pulsing, growing glory, ever given and ever renewed. Our glory is more like a song when it is sung and heard than when it is written on the score. The universe is the sound of God singing.

We participate in this only when we choose to. When we follow other gods, God does not compel us to return to him. We have often turned our backs on God, sometimes knowingly, sometimes unknowingly. But the result is always the same: we separate ourselves from God and the rest of his creation; our voices grow silent as the rest of creation sings its Creator's song; like an ember pulled from the fire, we grow dull and cold.

Lord, make us "worthy of our calling." When you listen to us, may you hear your own song, sung through our voices, not the dissonant noises of our own cryings and whinings. When you look at us, may you see the flesh you have made in your image, not the vanities we create in our own image. When you examine our thoughts and desires, may you find in them a will reflecting your own will, a will in harmony with all things, not the self-will that leads to destruction. Think on us not as we have made ourselves, severed from the rest of your creation, unable to sing and bear our part, but as you have restored us in Christ, changed from glory into glory, cloaked and shining with his love. Remember, Lord, not what we deserve, but what you have wrought in us.

Sometimes we do not know you, Lord. At other times we know you, but not enough to love you. At other times we love you, but not enough to serve you. At other times we serve you, but not enough to please you. Grant us so to know you that we cannot help but love you, so to love you that we cannot help but serve you, so to serve you that we cannot help but please you. Dwell in our minds that we may know you, in our hearts that we may love you, in our lives that we may serve you, and all that we may please you now and evermore. What we ask comes only as your gift to us. Grant us this gift always.

Tune Thou my harp;
There is not, Lord, could never be,
The skill in me.

Tune Thou my harp,
That it may play Thy melody,
Thy harmony.

Tune Thou my harp;
O Spirit, breathe Thy thought through me,
As pleaseth Thee.
(Amy Carmichael)

PROPER 2

With Free Hearts

Almighty and merciful God, in your goodness keep us, we pray, from all things that may hurt us, that we, being ready both in mind and body, may accomplish with free hearts those things which belong to your purpose.

I walk five miles each weekday, two and a half miles to work in the morning and two and a half miles home in the evening, and on weekends I often walk up Mount Adams, the hill behind my residence, a height of about six hundred feet. For most of my life, though, I ran two miles every day. It wasn't until my late fifties, when I was no longer lifting my feet as high as I once did and began tripping over broken pavement and uneven flagstones, that I switched to walking. Daily exercise has been, for all my adult life, very important to me.

I began the discipline of running while in college, at a time when I was getting no exercise and couldn't sleep at night. I knew

I needed to get into shape, and running seemed the simplest and quickest way to do it. I came to enjoy the benefits exercise brought me: a clearer mind, a more restful sleep, a more relaxed disposition. But I never enjoyed the running itself (as I do enjoy walking today). My heart and lungs strained when I ran. Sometimes it was almost as if they pleaded with me to stop. But I pressed on until I had run my distance. The strain I felt when running (and the strain I today feel when I walk to the top of Mount Adams) was strengthening my muscles to do what they could not otherwise do. Regular exercise keeps my body strong and healthy, freeing me to choose activities requiring strength and health. Those choices would otherwise be closed to me. I thank God for the gifts of strength and health and the freedom they afford me.

Exertion is good for the body; hurt is something else. When I am hurt, I can neither run nor walk, and many activities that I once enjoyed are no longer possible. My choices are narrowed, my freedom diminished.

As with the body, so with the soul. Regular spiritual exercise is sometimes a strain, calling for discipline and concentration. Sometimes our souls would rather sit idle. While idleness can refresh the soul and has its place, if it usurps the time of exercise, our souls grow flabby, and our spiritual freedom is diminished. We enjoy intimate communion with God only when we regularly and intentionally listen for his voice and respond to him. This requires a disciplined effort. When we grow slack in prayer, we cannot hear God, and if we cannot hear him, we cannot follow him. Then we are no longer free. Perfect freedom is service to God, giving ourselves to accomplish those things that belong to his purpose and to our nature. Such freedom is only possible for those who have taken the time and made the effort to listen for God's voice and know God's purposes.

In this prayer we ask God to keep us not from the strain that leads to spiritual freedom and obedience, but from the hurts that lead to spiritual captivity and listlessness. Even when our bodies grow infirm, our souls may remain vibrant, attentive, and obedient. Should this happen to us, we can do no better than to repeat the prayer of John Donne from his sickbed:

> O most mighty and most merciful God, who though thou have taken me off my feet, hast not taken me off my foundation, which is thyself, who though thou have removed me from that upright form, in which I could stand, and see thy throne, the heavens, yet hast not removed from me that light by which I can lie, and see thyself, who though thou have weakened my bodily knees, that they cannot bow to thee, hast yet left me the knees of my heart, which are bowed unto thee evermore; as thou hast made this bed, thine altar, make me thy sacrifice; and as thou makest thy Son Christ Jesus the priest, so make me his deacon, to minister to him in a cheerful surrender of my body, and soul to thy pleasure, by his hands. (*Devotions*, III, "Prayer")

PROPER 3

Joyfully Serve

Grant, O Lord, that the course of this world may be peaceably governed by your providence; and that your Church may joyfully serve you in confidence and serenity.

This prayer contains a two-part petition, the first for the world and the second for the church.

For the world, we pray for peaceable governing. The daily headlines and news clips seem to mock such a petition. Violence and injustice fester like incurable boils on the face of the world. While we may not be personally responsible for most of the world's ills, we are part of the scene and therefore part of everything else in the scene. Perhaps we are not ourselves victims, but neither do we exert ourselves on behalf of those who are. We pray for them. We send checks to agencies seeking their relief. We grimace and comment about the suffering of people in faraway places. But mostly, we sit idly by, spending our days in relative comfort, as if in a tranquil pool sheltered behind the bank of a roaring and polluted river. We may have known the river's swirling eddies in times past, but now we live beside quieter waters. The river rushes violently; we are restless and uneasy because we cannot block out the sound of it. We pray God to purify it and quiet its currents, to clean, chasten, discipline, and channel the river by his providence. Arouse yourself, Lord, to govern your world peaceably!

For the church, we pray for joyful service. Much of the service of God carried out by the church is less than joyful. The church seems too much a reflection of the world, beset with tensions resembling those seen elsewhere. Before the church can joyfully serve its Lord, two things must happen: we must stop taking ourselves so seriously, and we must take Christ more seriously.

Christians are sometimes deadly serious people. Some years ago, the television program *Saturday Night Live* featured a character called "Church Lady," played by Dana Carvey. This parody of a church worker was a popular feature of the show because most viewers had known someone very much like Church Lady: moralistic, humorless, compulsive, obsessed with the rules of religion. There was nothing joyful about Church Lady's serving the Lord, and one suspected that if a hint of joy had somehow intruded into her soul, she would have stamped it out. Church Lady sought to banish Satan from the world, but her joyless witness played into Satan's hands by making Christian faith appear unappealing.

Several years ago, when I became editor of a Christian newspaper, I sought to inject more humor into the paper's pages. I searched for someone who could write a regular column to help Christians laugh. Finding humorous material was easy, but the humor had an edge to it. Many people wrote hilarious pieces that made those on the other side of the theological fence appear foolish or unfaithful. Such humor was a means of attacking an opponent. Though it made me laugh, it was actually very serious and far from the spirit of Christ. Finally, I found a retired bishop from Tacoma, Washington, who could write winsome, tongue-in-cheek pieces about church life, poking harmless fun at everyone, beginning with himself. He had no axe to grind. His obvious enjoyment of life in the church and lack of rancor made his column a popular feature with many readers. But without fail, after each column appeared, I received several letters to the editor, angrily rebuking me for printing something that found humor in what the letter writer could only see as a deadly serious business. Joyless Christians, I concluded, abound in the church and are found on every side of every controversy.

This lack of humor in the church results from our taking ourselves too seriously. Our little systems take on the appearance of ultimacy in our minds. We begin to believe the kingdom will rise or fall depending on the fate of our point of view. It is not Christ who is Lord, but ourselves and our opinions. Because everything depends on our efforts, we cannot afford the time to stop and smile. As a result, those who might be drawn to Christ look at us and say, no, thank you.

Once we stop taking ourselves so seriously, we can begin to take Christ seriously. The first step is to acknowledge that however convinced we may be of this or that theological position, Christ transcends it. In Christ we confront an inexplicable paradox—a power infinitely beyond us, yet intimately present among and within us. Our tiny minds cannot comprehend such a mystery, and when we realize this, we begin to see how comic we are, passionately defending our answers when we haven't even understood the questions.

The next step leads to the "confidence and serenity" to which the prayer refers. We discover that we need not know the answers because Christ knows the answers, Christ loves us, and Christ is Lord. We learn that we can trust Christ, though we cannot understand him, though even in our most insightful moments, we trace but the outskirts of his ways. We find the darkness of our minds less threatening because we hear his voice in the darkness, we feel his touch, and we know he has traveled this way before us and tamed whatever demons lie ahead on the trail.

What, then, of the world and its peaceable governance? We don't have to know what our nation, our church, or we personally should do in Iraq, Afghanistan, or Palestine. We don't even have to know what should be done at the intersection down the street. We follow Christ as faithfully as we can. That means we must love God and our neighbor, acknowledging that those two categories encompass everyone and everything that is. This will affect (and probably change) everything we do, with the result that the small corner of the world where we live will be a bit more peaceably governed. As for the rest, we trust Jesus.

PROPER 4

Never-Failing Providence

O God, your never-failing providence sets in order all things both in heaven and earth: Put away from us, we entreat you, all hurtful things, and give us those things which are profitable for us.

The attribution in this prayer defines an often neglected element in the Christian view of life—divine providence. Providence is God's ordering of all things. Belief in divine providence leads to a vibrant confidence in the goodness of the world and the future.

This confidence is not a groundless optimism, a "Don't-worry-because-everything-will-be-all-right" denial of painful realities. It is, rather, a profound orientation of the soul, a way of understanding our lives and events around us, even when confusing and painful things occur.

I shall never forget the time several years ago when I was called to visit two parishioners in the hospital. They had been in automobile accidents the same day, sustained similar injuries, and been taken to the same hospital. When I walked into the first hospital room, my parishioner growled at me and said, "This could not have happened at a worse time. I've got important contracts to finalize, and now I'm cooped up in this damned hospital room. The nurses are surly, and the food awful. And all because that damned fool ran a stop sign. No, I don't feel like taking communion." I mumbled an expression of sympathy and left as soon as I could. When I entered the second room, my parishioner greeted me with a warm smile, and said, "I'm so glad to see you! I knew you'd come—it's been that kind of day. After the accident, an ambulance was on the scene in nearly no time, and they brought me here to this hospital where I know I'm in good hands. My partner has assured me he'll call me every day that I'm here and we'll be okay at the office. Oh, I see you brought me communion—thank you!"

Which parishioner had the "right" outlook on his circumstances? Some people would say the first man; others would say the second man. The two men looked for different things, and each found what he was looking for. Providence is God's goodness and power sustaining order and determining direction in the world about us. Don't try to prove that order and direction are there, because only those already inclined to see them will accept your proof.

Providence does not mean God determines everything that happens. Such a denial of human freedom is more akin to the ancient Greek belief in fate than the Christian belief in providence. Providence affirms that the course of history (and of individual lives within history) is not capricious or meaningless, but is

moving toward a goal, a culmination: history has a plot or plan.
Human freedom is part of this plot or plan, which means God has
allowed for things to go awry. He has also provided means to set
them right again.

It is as if we are swimming in a river. The river flows down-
stream. That has been determined and nothing we do will change
it. We can, however, decide whether we like the direction of the
current or not. We can swim against the current if we wish, and if
we're strong, we can maintain our anti-current direction for some
time. But in the end, along with everything else in the river, we will
arrive at the ocean.

Why does God allow people to swim against the current? If we
were in charge of the world, perhaps we wouldn't allow it. Things
would be much simpler if everyone cooperated with the divine
order. But I hear God whispering into my ear: *That shows how
little you know about my order. I suppose if you were ordering the
world, you'd eliminate war. How would you do it? By removing all the
weapons? Hateful people would invent new ones. By eliminating
hatred? But only a heart that is free to hate is free to love. I allow
people to defy me because I want them to* choose *to obey me; I allow
them to hate me because I want them to* choose *to love me.*"

But, Lord, it's so hard to believe your providence is "never-
failing" when so many people suffer!

"Don't you know anything, Dick? When people suffer, I suffer. *It's
not that I allow people to suffer while I go off and play golf. By
choosing to let people suffer, I choose to suffer myself. Their hunger,
desolation, and persecution are my own hunger, desolation, and
persecution. But if I eliminated suffering, I would also eliminate need,
your need for each other and your need for me. Without need, there
would be no giving. Without suffering, there would be no forgiveness.
Without pain, there would be no healing. Without sin, there would be
no grace. You would soon cease to care for one another and for me, and
perhaps I would cease to care for you, because no caring would be
called for. A self-sufficient and endless loneliness would descend upon
us all. Would that be an improvement?"*

No, Sir, I suppose not.

Proper 5

From Whom All Good Proceeds

O God, from whom all good proceeds: Grant that by your inspiration we may think those things that are right, and by your merciful guiding may do them.

All good proceeds from God. If we seek what is good, we must seek it from God, for good proceeds from no other source.

We usually seek it elsewhere. Sometimes we seek good in the results of our own labor. If we make enough phone calls, drive enough miles, knock on enough doors, read enough books, cook enough meals, pound enough nails, say enough prayers, we think we will find what is good. We would banish from our lives all that is unworthy and mean, and create the good through sheer force of effort. We then stare blankly at the walls, wondering why nothing gets better. We grow demoralized and exhausted.

Sometimes we seek good by building walls around ourselves to insulate us from what causes us discomfort. We drive our air-conditioned sedans along elevated freeways that block from our view the sultry tenements and languid streets below. We dine at exclusive clubs and lay down our heads at night on down pillows in barricaded houses. But our sleep is restless and we are not refreshed. Rich in things and poor in soul, we grow demoralized and exhausted.

Sometimes we seek good through the myriad little therapies of our time that urge us to this or that new height of self-fulfillment, to reach our full potential, to take care of ourselves. And when at last the heights are attained, our potential reached, our selves cared for, we turn around and wonder about the purpose of it all. Is there nothing more? Is that all there is? We grow demoralized and exhausted.

We have forgotten that the source of all good is not in ourselves. Good flows from God and is ours as a gift from God. We claim the gift by attentive obedience, and once we accept it, our minds disengage from trying to find or create it. We become grateful for the gift received and seek ways to embody that gift in our lives.

This embodying of good in our lives is part of God's gift. It begins with our thoughts, then determines our actions. God inspires our minds and guides our behaviors, like wind that transforms a pennant hanging limp from the pole into a rippling banner and causes silent wind chimes to sing. The power is not our own, but its effect is manifest in us.

We continue to pray for this inspiration and guidance, that we may exhibit more fully every day the good that comes from God. But gradually, our prayer becomes less an asking for what is lacking and more a thanksgiving for what is already given, already received, already enjoyed. We know that we shall at times slip back into the old habits, seeking the good in ourselves and in things, growing once more demoralized and exhausted. The powers of hell will not let us forget entirely the old ways. But now we recognize them for the dead-end avenues they have always been. We know the source of the good and that the source never ceases to give all good things to those who love him.

Thank you, good and gracious God, for leading us to see the fruitlessness of trusting in ourselves and in the things about us. Thank you for leading us to a new trust in you as the source of all that is good. Guide our thoughts and inspire our actions. As you have done in the past, do more and more in the future, that day by day, our prayer may grow ever more subsumed in thankfulness and praise.

PROPER 6

Your Household the Church

*Keep, O Lord, your household the Church in your steadfast
faith and love, that through your grace we may proclaim your
truth with boldness, and minister your justice with compassion.*

Clergy are fond of referring to their parishes as "the parish
family," intending, I suppose, to suggest the image of "one big,
happy family." But no family or household is always united, always
big, always happy. Even the healthiest family travels through a
range of experiences; even the most "functional" family is dysfunc-
tional now and then. Good times are hoped for, but households are
not always pleasant places.

In calling the church God's household, this prayer suggests
to us a complex set of relationships and experiences, involving
dependence and independence, loyalty and betrayal, joy and grief,
industry and laziness, kindness and thoughtlessness, profundity
and pettiness. This is the nature of a household; it is also the nature
of the church.

The prayer defines the church's task: to proclaim God's truth
with boldness and minister God's justice with compassion. It is a
job for which we are not qualified and that we cannot do. We have
only two choices: give up or ask for help. In praying this collect,
we are asking for help.

But before we can minister God's justice with compassion, we
must, as the prayer says, reside in God's faith and love. Here we
entrust ourselves to God's faith and love, which we do not hesitate

to call steadfast. This is not the same as asking God to strengthen our own faith and love, though we pray for that as well.

It seems odd to speak of God's faith—in what or in whom does God have faith? God has faith in us because he made us and knows our capabilities. It is like a craftsman's faith in his hammer and chisel—the craftsman knows what his hammer and chisel can do. In this prayer, we say to God, "Do not give up on us. Bear with us still. Keep faith in us. Remember what you can do in us despite our flaws and infidelities." And God will not give up on us. Even if we give up on God, God will not give up on us. This is a prayer granted even before it is uttered.

God's steadfast love is surely not an easy love for God. When a parent watches a daughter or son slip into self-destructive habits and company, the parent grieves. When a husband or wife watches a mate dishonor the marriage vow, the husband or wife grieves. When God watches us worship our golden calves and build our towers of Babel, God grieves. But God will not stop loving us, because he cannot. There are very few things God cannot do, but to stop loving us is one of them. We are therefore praying for something that God cannot help but grant.

How, then, do we proclaim the truth with boldness? Simply to know the truth often seems difficult. Many of us have been certain we knew the truth, that God had unveiled himself and his plans to us, only to find later that the matter was more complex than we realized. We learned humility when we proclaimed the truth boldly and then discovered that what we proclaimed was something other than the whole, pure truth. We then grew hesitant to proclaim anything boldly again. Our problem is that we misunderstand the nature of the truth. We think it is doctrines or ideas or moral dicta. But truth is not a proposition; it is a relationship with a person. "*I* am the way, and the truth, and the life," Jesus said (John 14:6). We proclaim Jesus by pointing to him as John the Baptist did. We proclaim Jesus by introducing people to him as Andrew did to his brother Simon. Then Jesus speaks for himself—and we are often surprised by what he says. How can we find the means to point to Jesus and introduce people to him? Ask for the means.

And how do we minister justice with compassion? Our tendency is either to minister justice (to make certain that everyone gets what he deserves) or to be compassionate (to make excuses for people's wrong behaviors). To minister God's justice is not to decide who deserves what, but to act justly ourselves, by dealing fairly and generously with one another and the rest of creation. And to act compassionately is to refuse to judge another person, however contrary to the will of God we may believe him to have behaved. If scores must be settled, God will settle them. It is not our place even to suggest what scores need settling. How can we find the means to stop judging God's children? Ask for the means.

PROPER 7

Perpetual Love and Reverence

O Lord, make us have perpetual love and reverence for your holy Name, for you never fail to help and govern those whom you have set upon the sure foundation of your loving-kindness.

The contemporary version of this prayer replaces the traditional word *fear* with *reverence*. This is like adding water to soup: the taste is much the same, only weaker. The word *reverence* too often suggests to the modern ear the outward shell of religion, as when parents enjoin their children to show "reverence" in church, meaning they should sit still, or when someone "reverences" the altar with a slight bow.

The stronger word *fear* is better, even with the connotation of evil that it sometimes carries. God is not evil. The fear with which we approach God has nothing to do with divine malevolence. It is more like the fear we feel of an earthquake or a tornado. These are not evil powers, but they are beyond our control or manipulation. We must come to terms with them as they are; there is no compromising or bargaining. We prepare ourselves to confront them by building our houses carefully, laying in a store of the right supplies, and being ready to meet them at any moment.

Our fear of God is like that. When we try to compromise with God ("Let's redefine our terms in the light of modern reality") or strike a bargain with God ("If you will grant me this, I promise to. . . "), we show that we have lost any fear of God. God becomes a mere pal, to be approached as an equal, with a set of terms to which we expect God to adjust and respond. This is dangerous behavior, as Job learned after he demanded that God appear to answer Job's questions. The Lord came to Job out of the midst of a tornado with his own set of questions.

But side by side with our fear of God stands our love of God. It is a love born of mystery, beauty, and wonder, not unrelated to our fear of God. Awful and overpowering though we find God to be, we are also strangely drawn to God, as filings are drawn to a magnet. It is as if we inhaled a delicious scent in the air and found ourselves moving irresistibly toward its source. We find God alluring, appealing, attractive. We want to surrender to God—yet we hold back. Can we be certain of God? Other things allure us as well; we are confused; our hearts and minds are divided.

There can be no certainty until the act of commitment has been made. We often try to enter a relationship with God that resembles a "trial marriage." The trouble with a trial marriage is that it isn't a marriage and it isn't like a marriage. People living together without commitment experience something other than marriage. Marriage can be known only from within. It makes all the difference when each partner knows the other will be true even when one's behavior might make ending the marriage an enticing notion. God never fails to help those who are set on the sure foundation of his loving-kindness, but until we stand on that foundation, we cannot be sure of it. Even afterward, doubts and fears will dart through our minds from time to time, but we do not fall because our foundation is sure.

It is in Jesus Christ that God emerges from Job's tornado and in whom the foundation of God's loving-kindness is visible. The wind still blows; the power and majesty of God are not compromised. But in the midst of the wind we make out the lines of the face of Jesus, who invites us to come to him that he may hold us in his arms.

. ☙ .

PROPER 8

The Foundation of the Apostles and Prophets

Almighty God, you have built your Church upon the foundation of the apostles and prophets, Jesus Christ himself being the chief cornerstone: Grant us so to be joined together in unity of spirit by their teaching, that we may be made a holy temple acceptable to you.

So then you are no longer strangers and sojourners, but you are fellow citizens with the saints and members of the household of God, built upon the foundation of the apostles and prophets, Christ Jesus himself being the cornerstone, in whom the whole structure is joined together and grows into a holy temple in the Lord; in whom you also are built into it for a dwelling place of God in the Spirit. (Ephesians 2:19—22)

The attribution in this prayer should not be overlooked: God has built the church. We can imagine the prayer beginning differ-

Almighty God, we have built your Church. . . . " This is, in fact, what we often think. We act as if the responsibility for building the church rests on our shoulders: establishing priorities, setting goals and objectives, erecting and maintaining buildings, raising money, developing strategies, programs, ministries, and activities. These things are important, but the church does not stand or fall depending upon how industrious, creative, clever, or articulate we are. God is the builder of the church. He works through us in many instances, and our role is therefore a noble one. But sometimes he works in spite of us. When we forget who is in charge, we become an obstacle for God to overcome, and one of two things happens: our projects succeed, but God is not in them; or our projects fail while God goes about his work without us.

God has built his church upon the foundation of the apostles and prophets. This foundation is more than a congenial fellowship of like-minded people. Those seeking pleasant company may find it in the church, but pleasant company can be sought elsewhere, and with fewer questions asked. Church life is sometimes less than cordial, and if congenial fellowship were what held the church together, it would have dissolved centuries ago.

Some Christians see the foundation of the apostles and prophets as the doctrinal statements coming to us from the scriptures and the patristic period. Such statements are important in that they set the intellectual and moral boundaries beyond which it is dangerous to stray, but their importance is secondary and derivative. Bickering among Christians is usually over these secondary matters. This occurs when Christians lose sight of the fundamental reality, which is love and faithfulness to God, the builder of the church. That love and faithfulness is what binds the church in one. It is "the foundation of the apostles and prophets." Without it, doctrinal orthodoxy avails nothing.

I recall the professor, a prim Englishman named A. Denis Baly, who taught me the Bible during my undergraduate years at Kenyon College. I developed a warm friendship with Denis Baly and was often in his home. As my teacher, he led me beyond the Sunday school religion of my childhood into a mature understanding of biblical doctrine. By graduation, I was able to relate what all the apostles and prophets had said about God. Over forty years later, I still carry with me the ideas I learned from Denis Baly, and those ideas still guide my understanding of the scriptures. But Denis Baly's chief legacy to me was neither his friendship nor the ideas he taught me, but the passion for the God of the Bible that I heard in his voice and saw in his eyes. That passion for God was contagious, and it flows through my veins to this day.

Denis Baly was a kind of apostle or prophet in my life. The chief thing we learn from apostles and prophets is passion for God. It is not the things they say and write, the fire of God in their hearts is the basis for the church's unity; it is this that makes us "a holy temple."

Jesus Christ is the chief cornerstone, "in whom the whole structure is joined together and grows," as St. Paul says. Paul may have had in mind the headstone of an arch, which bears the arch's weight. Christ is also the foundation. The foundation of a building determines its shape and supports its walls. The prayer, following Paul, refers to the apostles and prophets as the foundation, but they are the church's foundation only in that they lead us to Christ, through whom love and faithfulness to God become possible. Jesus Christ is "the church's one foundation."

PROPER 9

Loving You and Our Neighbor

O God, you have taught us to keep all your commandments by loving you and our neighbor: Grant us the grace of your Holy Spirit, that we may be devoted to you with our whole heart, and united to one another with pure affection.

So many questions: Are loving God and loving our neighbor different things or two ways of saying the same thing? What is love, and is it possible to love someone whom we do not like? Is love like respect? Like honor? Like passion? It is more than a feeling, but is it related to feelings? Is it possible to be exhausted, bored, disgusted, neglectful, hurtful, but still love?

Christ has taught us that the commandments are summarized in love of God and neighbor (Matthew 22:37–39). He taught this not so much by precept as by example. Looking at the example he gave us, how would we answer those perplexing questions about the meaning of love?

First, loving God and loving our neighbor are not different things, but the same thing. Love sees everything in relation to everything else—God, our neighbor, ourselves, all things. All of creation is like an orchestra, the individual creatures like instruments. The symphony soars through the air into the listener's ear when all the instruments play their parts according to the score. Not all instruments are the same and not all are equal. Sameness and equality would interfere with the music and are not part of love; mutual need and respect are.

God is the composer of the score, the conductor of the orchestra, the inventor and maker of the instruments, the architect and builder of the music hall. Love acknowledges a mutual dependence of all created things on one another (one flute or viola cannot play the symphony alone), and a dependence of the whole upon God, whose vision and vitality give rise to the music and sustain it.

Second, love is a vision lived. It is not merely an awareness in the mind of the relatedness of all things, but a moment-to-moment choosing to live as part of the whole. We like people with whom we share a common interest, but liking has nothing to do with choosing to live as part of the whole.

Third, respect and honor are essential parts of love. As a man, Christ respected and honored all creation, especially those who received no honor and respect from other sources. Christ respected and honored even those who did not respect and honor others.

Passion is also part of love because passion affirms relatedness. Christ wept over Lazarus. He raved at the hypocrites. He rebuked demons. But none of us can feel equal passion for all people. Passion is also unsustainable and exhausting. Therefore exhaustion must be part of love as well.

Boredom? Did people ever bore Jesus? I recall no such occasion in the Gospels. I suppose love always sees beyond the trivial conversation of the moment, the story repeated for the tenth time, the preoccupation with banalities. Behind all these, love detects and connects with a person whose joys, fears, uncertainties, and longings are part of God's master plan. Love sees a reflection of God in everyone and everything, and that, I suppose, is why we have no indication that anyone ever bored Jesus.

Disgust? Yes, Christ grew disgusted with behaviors and attitudes that denied mutual need and respect, and, I think, with persons who embodied those behaviors and attitudes. Love does not exclude disgust.

Neglect and hurtfulness? These, too, are compatible with love, but not with perfect love, not with Christ's love. I know them to be compatible with love because I recognize them in myself and

I know that I love those whom I sometimes hurt and neglect, including Christ himself. Hurt and neglect may deface love, but they cannot blot it out. My love for Christ is, in this respect, like my love for my wife. I have hurt and neglected her, my finest intentions and most solemn vows notwithstanding. Yet, I continue to love her, and she continues to love me. I promise to be faithful to her because I love her and she loves me. Day by day, I seek to live out all that is contained in that promise. Some days I keep my promise; perhaps in time I shall keep it without fail. So, too, God continues to love us, and we respond by promising in return to love God and our neighbor. Perhaps in time, by God's grace, we shall keep it without fail.

PROPER 10

Know and Understand

O Lord, mercifully receive the prayers of your people who call upon you, and grant that they may know and understand what things they ought to do, and also may have grace and power faithfully to accomplish them.

We call upon God for what we need and long for, and God has promised to hear our call: "Ask, and it will be given you; seek, and you will find; knock, and it will be opened to you. . . . What man of you, if his son asks him for bread, will give him a stone?. . . How much more will your Father who is in heaven give good things to those who ask him!" (Matthew 7:7–11).

Why must we ask? It is not because God is unaware of our

needs. It is not because God grants us his grace only in response to a formal request. As a father, I give my children what they need, whether they ask or not, whether they know their need or not, and God is more, not less, of a father than I.

We need not want the gift in order to receive it. Often God's grace comes to us when we do not want it, ask for it, or feel a need for it. Those are the times we are farthest from God, too blind to see our need, too lazy to ask if we had seen it. Those are the times God bludgeons us with the gift we need, and only then do we ask. God first gives his gift; our asking is the response. We call upon God as an acknowledgment of gifts already received (though perhaps unsought), and as an expression of our willingness to receive again at his hands.

We pray that we may know and understand what we are to do. Merely to do the right thing without knowledge and understanding is not enough. This is because what God desires from us is more than obedience; it is a relationship. It is the difference between a servant and a friend. "No longer do I call you servants, for the servant does not know what his master is doing; but I have called you friends" (John 15:15). By knowledge and understanding we become colleagues, partners, comrades, confidants. We share our master's goals, dreams, hopes, and sorrows. We enter into his soul and are privy to his master plan.

The knowledge and understanding we ask for begin with knowledge of ourselves—our rebellious self-will, our unworthiness to be considered a friend of God. We then move to knowledge of God—his love and acceptance of us despite our unworthiness. And finally comes the knowledge that although we do not deserve it and cannot see it clearly, God has a place for us.

With this knowledge that God accepts us and has a place for us, comes the awareness that he accepts others on the same terms. The professor who lectures brilliantly on the scriptures knows and understands himself and that God has a place for him. So also does the custodian who sweeps the classroom floor after the students and professor have departed. The professor and the custodian also know this about each other. Each seeks to do only what he is called to do, to take his place in God's plan, neither demeaning those whose callings the world regards as beneath his own, nor envying those whose callings the world regards as above his own. Notions of higher and lower are human, not divine, and they exist only in the eye of those who do not know the master's plan.

Finally, we pray for the grace and power to do what we are called to do. It is God who works in us to accomplish his will. When we pray, "Thy will be done," we acknowledge that God will work his purpose out. We do not work it out. Sometimes God works out his purpose through us, sometimes in spite of us. It makes no difference in the end—God will work his purpose out— but it makes all the difference to us whether we are instruments whom God uses or obstacles whom God overcomes.

PROPER 11

Our Ignorance in Asking

Almighty God, the fountain of all wisdom, you know our necessities before we ask and our ignorance in asking: Have compassion on our weakness, and mercifully give us those things which for our unworthiness we dare not, and for our blindness we cannot ask; through the worthiness of your Son Jesus Christ our Lord.

Years ago, I had been rector of a small parish for several years. I enjoyed the people but wanted a larger challenge. I prayed that God would open the right door for me. One day I was offered a position that seemed a dream come true. The new position called for me to move to a large city and undertake work I envisioned as exciting because it would enable me to grow in new ways. The salary and benefits were large. Others saw it as a plum assignment. With confidence in my stride, I accepted the new position. It was an answer to my prayers, I thought.

In the years that followed, I grew increasingly unhappy in my new position, finally concluding it hadn't been what I needed after all—it had been merely what I wanted. Emerging from the depression shrouding my soul, I began to see that what I needed was something very different. I needed to be still and let God enfold me in his arms. Finally, I resigned my job and took another position that paid less, but in which God restored joy to my soul. Perhaps in allowing me to accept a position that would drive me to him, God had given me what I needed after all, although it was hardly what I had asked for. I had been right about one thing: the position led me to grow in new ways, though not the ways I had anticipated.

Other people have had similar experiences. They exhausted themselves building a business, a church, a reputation, a career, or a fortune, only to discover that what they had pursued so intently was merely a desire, not a need; all their striving had left them feeling emptier than before. Many of these people also perceived, as I did, that God had been leading them into and through the darkness, until they came to their senses and turned to him, saying, "I no longer ask for anything but you, Lord. Come and fill me. Make me your temple, and never depart from me."

We do not know even what to ask for. Starving, we think we are full. We mistake acquaintance for intimacy, association for community. Surrounded by things, we are barren within. Lost, we have forgotten that we had a destination. We confuse desire with need. Our desires vary, but they commonly include money, possessions, power, prestige, popularity, health, beauty, and sex. Like runners chasing a finish line that keeps moving, we grow exhausted and cynical. If we are religious, we may pray for strength to carry on, sometimes overlaying our desires with a veneer of nobility, telling ourselves we do it for our family, for a better community, or for God. But the more we acquire, the more we want, and still we feel empty inside. We discover that "enough" is forever out of reach.

We stand before the Lord like treasonous soldiers. We have not listened or obeyed our Lord. We have followed our own fancies and do not deserve pardon, still less reinstatement. We therefore offer our prayer through the worthiness of Christ, who says to us, *"I will intercede for you. You do not know how to pray, so I will pray for you and through you. You must say nothing, do nothing. Be still as I begin to speak and act in you. Expect to be surprised. I know your needs, before you ask and whether or not you ask. True prayer begins with me, flows through me and out from me, and then returns to me."*

> Eternal Spirit of the living Christ,
> I know not how to ask or what to say;
> I only know my need, as deep as life,
> and only you can teach me how to pray.
>
> Come, pray in me the prayer I need this day;
> help me to see your purpose and your will
> where I have failed, what I have done amiss,
> held in forgiving love, let me be still.
> (*Hymnal 1982*, #698)

PROPER 12

Things Temporal . . . Things Eternal

O God, the protector of all who trust in you, without whom nothing is strong, nothing is holy: Increase and multiply upon us your mercy; that, with you as our ruler and guide, we may so pass through things temporal, that we lose not the things eternal.

The petition of this prayer asks that we may pass through things temporal and lose not the things eternal. There is a danger in becoming overly attached to things temporal and forgetting that we merely pass through them to the things eternal. Our permanent address is elsewhere.

But there is more to it than that. We must not think of this as a derogatory statement about things temporal. Some Christians have tended toward a Platonic dualism, denigrating the things of this world, especially physical pleasures, as evil and opposed to things of the spirit. Christian living then becomes having as little as possible to do with things temporal. But God is the Creator of all things and all things are therefore good. While not being captivated by them, we are to pay close attention to things temporal, even to enjoy them.

When teaching in Nigeria several years ago, I had occasion to preach on 2 Corinthians 4:18 which says: "[B]ecause we look not at what can be seen but at what cannot be seen." In my sermon I coupled that verse with 1 John 4:20: "[F]or those who do not love a brother or sister whom they have seen, cannot love God whom

they have not seen." The first verse seems to say (as this prayer
seems to say) that we should focus on unseen things, presumably
God and heaven. The second verse says if we aren't right with the
person near at hand whom we can see, we may as well forget about
being right with God whom we cannot see. I posed this question
in my sermon: What is a Christian's primary concern? Is it to keep
heaven, the unseen reality, in view, or is it to live faithfully in our
day-to-day relationships in this world? I said the scriptures and the
spiritual masters of Christian history can be cited to support both
views.

Then I compared America with Nigeria: "My country is an
increasingly this-worldly society," I said. "That has resulted in
major advances in communications, manufacturing, agriculture,
medicine, transportation, and education. It was made possible by a
brilliantly conceived political constitution written by people with
their eyes on this world, a constitution designed to protect the
citizens from abuses of power. But America is in danger of losing
her soul because many Americans no longer see their lives rooted
in an unseen transcendent reality. Doubt and anxiety are endemic
in America. Nigeria, on the other hand, is a country where
virtually everyone, whether Muslim, Christian, or of a traditional
religion, takes for granted that he is in relationship to a transcendent reality. Religious doubt is, so far as I can see, unknown here.
But I have heard too many sermons in Nigeria that end with the
facile assurance that 'God will deliver us from our troubles.'
Perhaps God wants Nigerians to make the hard and challenging
decisions required to rid the country of corruption and tyranny.
Belief in God does not absolve human beings of taking responsibility for their lives. If America needs more other-worldliness,
Nigeria needs more this-worldliness." We face twin temptations,
one to dwell entirely on this world and the other to dwell
entirely on the next world. It is possible to veer off course in
either direction.

When my wife and I lived in West Virginia, we enjoyed
driving the back roads of that beautiful state. Occasionally we
came across an old, wooden covered bridge. Once we entered the

bridge, the sky and countryside were temporarily blocked from view, creating the illusion that the small space within the bridge was all the space there was. We had to heed what happened inside the bridge so as not to run into other vehicles or the walls of the bridge itself. We could not pass through the bridge without concerning ourselves with our immediate environment. But the bridge was not our home. We drove carefully across the bridge but we kept our eyes on the light at the far end of the bridge that grew brighter as we approached it. We were on the bridge because we were traveling to a destination beyond the bridge, and the bridge was the way to get there. We would have been in trouble if we had not paid attention to the bridge, but we did not preoccupy ourselves with it and we did not tarry on it.

I am also reminded of the four years I spent in college. College is intended to be like driving through the covered bridge. A student passes through college on the way to adulthood, and a college education is preparation for the joys and responsibilities of adulthood. Life on campus contains everything that the student will later find in the adult world: challenging personal relationships, choices, conflict, discipline, temptation, joy, sorrow, success, failure, doubt, faith, growth. By learning to deal with these things in college, the student prepares for adult life.

Similarly, things temporal equip our souls for eternity. They change us, mold us, prepare us for eternity, and leave their imprint on us for eternity. It is not only permissible but intended that we enjoy these temporal things. God provides them not only for our growth but for our delight as well. The question is whether, as we pass through them, we will recognize them for what they are and use them to prepare ourselves for what lies beyond. If we focus exclusively on things temporal, they become a hindrance rather than a preparation for eternity. We are to enjoy and give thanks for them but not be captivated by them. With the things of this world, we are to be like Teflon, not Velcro.

PROPER 13

Cleanse and Defend Your Church

Let your continual mercy, O Lord, cleanse and defend your Church; and, because it cannot continue in safety without your help, protect and govern it always by your goodness.

This is a prayer for the health and soundness of the church. What ails the church? Of what maladies does the church need healing? The chief ailment of the church is what it has always been: false worship. When we in the church look upon our doctrines and experiences as ultimate truths, the standard by which everything is to be judged, we worship control. Since we are the ones who know the truth, we must be in control: other people must learn from us, not we from them. Our experiences and beliefs become idols. We become like people whose knowledge of the sea consists of a walk along the beach and a few stories about fishing— and who then presume to deliver lectures on oceanography. It is not that their knowledge is wrong. It is accurate as far as it goes, but it is incomplete. When such people come to see that others have experienced the ocean in ways unknown to them, they recognize other points of view not as opposed to their own, but as complementary to their own, and their own experiences and beliefs cease to be idols.

The outward trappings of religion often support this idolatry by inflating the church's sense of itself. They seem to speak of power and influence—not God's, but ours. Gold-gilded vestments, soaring gothic arches, fancy processions, honorific titles for the clergy—when kept in perspective, these things may enhance the church's mission and ministry, but it is hard to keep them in perspective.

The church member (or congregation or denomination) who worships his own sense of control often becomes defensive when his self-importance is threatened. He can be a sad, pitiable figure. Or he can be infuriating. Or he can appear ridiculous, even comic, like the clown who prances solemnly about while others are amused at his foolishness. The comic dimension can be the beginning of conversion: when a self-important Christian comes to see the humor in himself, redemption is close at hand.

False worship is rarely the worship of something evil. Rather than tempt the church with conspicuous evil, Satan usually takes a secondary good and suggests to us that it is more important than everything else. It is a short step from this to the conclusion that we must take charge to defend this secondary good and defeat everyone and everything that would undermine it.

The parish where I served in the 1990s constructed a new church building. In preparing the congregation for this project, our lay leaders led us through several exercises to determine what was important in constructing a new church. At first, architectural style and appearance outweighed everything else in the minds of most of us. We each had an ideal structure in mind, usually based on some fondly remembered church from childhood, and many of us were prepared to insist on the church we envisioned. Our leaders, however, guided us to see that individual architectural preferences were secondary things. They helped us begin thinking instead about the One we worship, why we came together, and what kind of architectural space would elevate our worship. The architectural design we finally developed was based on these discussions, and although it doesn't look quite like the church any of us had in mind when we began, it serves its purpose well, and the congregation was happily united throughout the project. The reason, I think, was that we kept the primary thing in view.

Not every experience in church life is that happy. Secondary things often become primary in churches: worship times, what hymns to sing, whether to allow an outside group to use the church facilities, what rites to use, how to spend money, how to raise money, whether to hire a new staff member, whether to fire an old staff member, what color to paint the Sunday school rooms, whether to place a memorial plaque on the wall, what curriculum to buy, whether to amend the by-laws. Disputes at the diocesan and national levels are also usually about secondary things. Beneath every such dispute lurks the question of *who is in charge*. When a decision degenerates into a struggle for control, Satan is in charge, regardless of how the decision turns out. Only when we become willing to see the other side carry the day, and then to praise God for working his will, can we say that Christ is in charge. The primary thing must always be faithfulness to Christ. That means we must continually surrender our own wills and convictions to Christ. It is not important who gets his way, so long as Christ is in charge. Faithfulness to Christ is *the* primary thing; everything else is secondary.

PROPER 14

Cannot Exist without You

Grant to us, Lord, we pray, the spirit to think and do always those things that are right, that we, who cannot exist without you, may by you be enabled to live according to your will.

Seated in the darkness of a movie theater, we are drawn into the drama on the screen. Automobiles screech through city streets. Sirens scream. Gunfire breaks out. Characters whom the earlier scenes of the film have made us love or hate chase one another to see who will prevail. We feel ourselves caught up in what is happening before our eyes. We care about the outcome. It is as if all these exciting things are happening to us.

But of course they are not happening at all. The people we see are mere images. The power that sustains them is not their own. They are projections onto the screen from a light bulb shining through a lens in the rear of the theater. It is not that the light in the projector "created" the figures on the screen at a point in time and then allowed them to continue on their own power. The figures have no power. They are continually created by the light, sustained in their existence moment to moment by a power not their own. If the light in the projector were to burn out or the projector were to be unplugged, the figures would not merely cease to move—they would cease to exist.

The biblical doctrine of creation is not about what God *did* when the universe began, but about what God *is doing* as the universe continues. Human beings could not continue in existence, even as inanimate objects, without God's creative power. Creation is a continual outpouring of divine energy. If God were to turn his back on the universe, even for an instant, things would not merely stop moving—they would vanish, leaving no trace. Our dependence upon God is absolute.

But while we cannot live without God, we can and often do live without knowing God. This prayer therefore does not stop with acknowledging that we cannot live without God, but also asks for the spirit to think and do what is right, to live according to God's will.

The reference to God's will suggests that God is something more than a cosmic light bulb projecting images onto a screen. Of all the things in creation, the one most like God is not a light bulb, but a person. Persons enter into relationships with other persons. Within a personal relationship, one experiences desire, love, hate, pain, sacrifice, laughter, betrayal, forgiveness, joy. An old school of philosophy once thought of God as changeless and passionless, but such a God would be very unlike the God of the Bible, and impossible to resist, obey, hate, love, or pray to. An impossible God wouldn't seek out a relationship with human beings, and, from our vantage point, wouldn't be worth seeking out a relationship with. Such a God would, in fact, resemble a light bulb.

Ron DelBene has said that in the Bible, the word usually translated as *will* can also be translated as *yearning*. The expression "will of God" suggests to most people a list of rules or behaviors that God desires us to obey, as does the expression "those things that are right" from the petition of this prayer. Rules or behaviors could exist independently of God and one could, theoretically, obey them without reference to God. But the expression "yearning of God" suggests not a behavior, but an orientation of the heart. If God has a yearning for us rather than a will for us, then it's we ourselves God cares about, not what we do or don't do.

It's like the difference between the way a woman feels about the man who seeks to seduce her and the man who loves her. The seducer seeks to gratify his own desires and cares only what the woman can do for him. He cares nothing for the woman herself. She is guarded in his presence and does not reveal to him her deepest thoughts and feelings. There is no joy or security for her in knowing such a man. But when a woman knows that a man loves her, she feels free to reveal everything to him and finds joy and security in doing so, knowing that he cares not about what she can do for him, but what he can do for *her*—he yearns for her.

While I expect it does us good to ponder the will of God and to ask what God wants us to do with our lives, let us also remember God's yearning, the desire God has for us. We cannot live without God because he sustains us with his power every moment of our lives—but why does he do this? It has more to do with who we are than with what we do. God is less interested in our acts of obedience than in the pleasure of our company.

PROPER 15

A Sacrifice for Sin . . .
An Example of Godly Life

*Almighty God, you have given your only Son to be for us a
sacrifice for sin, and also an example of godly life: Give us
grace to receive thankfully the fruits of his redeeming work,
and to follow daily in the blessed steps of his most holy life.*

This prayer contains a couplet of nouns in the attribution—
sacrifice and example—and a couplet of verbs in the
petition—receive and follow. The movement of the prayer is from
Christ's work to our response. The reference to the crucifixion,
which sets the tone for the entire prayer, is the only such reference
in the Collects for the Church Year after the Easter season.

When I reflect on Christ's giving of himself as a sacrifice for
sin, my head and my heart make their approach from different
places. My head analyzes, asks theoretical questions: How was
Jesus' death a sacrifice for sin? Did Jesus have to die? If so, was it
to save us from our sins? If so, how did his death save us from our
sins? Was it a price paid? If so, to whom? And anyway, what does
it mean to be "saved from our sins?" These are trick questions.
They have answers, I'm sure, but the answers are too deep for me.
If I dwell upon them, my mind ties itself into knots.

My heart, on the other hand, doesn't analyze, and the questions
it asks are of a different sort. My heart envisions the scenes of the
story, with me as a participant. Jesus weeps in the Garden of
Gethsemane; I stand off to the side wringing my hands. Jesus is

tried before Pilate; I crouch in a corner, glancing nervously about.
Jesus screams, "My God, my God, why have you forsaken me?"
(Matthew 27:46). I wonder whether God has forsaken me as well,
and whether I have forsaken God. Jesus is offered vinegar to drink;
I start to offer water from my canteen, but am afraid and draw
back. Jesus speaks to the penitent thief; I want to say to him,
"Speak to me, too, Jesus! Speak to me!" Jesus dies; I cry.

Was I there when they crucified my Lord? Yes, in my heart
I was there. I saw love, oozing in sticky red drops:

> See, from his head, his hands, his feet,
> sorrow and love flow mingled down!
> Did e'er such love and sorrow meet,
> or thorns compose so rich a crown?
> (*Hymnal 1982*, #474)

Dying is not necessarily an act of love. But Jesus died voluntar-
ily, when he could have summoned a squadron of angels to rescue
him. In obedience and humility, he set aside the last trace of
respectability, of equality with God. A victim of crucifixion either
bled to death or slowly strangled as the weight of his body tight-
ened the muscles in his throat and cut off his windpipe. Jesus hangs
there, looks down at me, and says, *"Remember that I love you."*

Jesus' "sacrifice for sin" and his "example of godly life" are not
two separate things but the same thing. His final act of love on the
cross was the culmination of a life of love, expressed in obedience
and humility, like the final tonic chord into which a harmonic
progression resolves itself and comes to rest.

F. A. Iremonger tells of the time when the late Archbishop
William Temple preached at Oxford University in 1931. In the
darkest days of the Great Depression and with religious skepticism
and indifference in vogue among the intelligentsia, Temple spoke
to a packed house in St. Mary's Church every night for a week.
Students and faculty stood against the walls and sat in the aisles
and on the pulpit steps to hear the famous preacher. Some had
come for inspiration; many had come out of curiosity. The last

night of the mission, Temple was ready to ask for a commitment. The congregation was roaring out Isaac Watts's great hymn, "When I survey the wondrous cross" (from which the lines above are taken). But Temple stopped the singing before the last stanza and said, "I want you to read over this verse before you sing it. They are tremendous words. If you mean them with all your hearts, sing them as loud as you can. If you don't mean them at all, keep silent. If you mean them even a little, and want to mean them more, sing them very softly." There was dead silence as every eye fastened on the words printed on the songsheet. A moment later, the evening ended with two thousand voices singing in a whisper:

Were the whole realm of nature mine,
that were an offering far too small;
love so amazing, so divine,
demands my soul, my life, my all.
(*Hymnal 1982*, #474)

PROPER 16

Gathered Together in Unity

Grant, O merciful God, that your Church, being gathered together in unity by your Holy Spirit, may show forth your power among all peoples, to the glory of your Name.

Mention "the church" to someone on the street, and you're likely to be asked, "Which church?" The question is more than a question: it is a statement about Christian witness in the modern world. That witness is not a united one. "The church" believes, says, and does many things, some of which seem incompatible or contradictory. Labels abound in the church, and the purpose of labels is to distinguish one thing from another.

Denominationalism is the most obvious division within the church. Episcopalians, Congregationalists, Presbyterians, Quakers, Methodists, Baptists, Roman Catholics—the historic communions of America's founders—are only the most obvious of these denominational groupings. The historic churches often get along better with one another than they do with the splinter groups that have sprung from them. Add to these churches the growing number of Pentecostal churches, and the scene begins to resemble a huge car lot, with sedans, convertibles, station wagons, pick-ups, sports cars, vans—something for every customer. Christian unity gives way to an individualism that discounts our common devotion to Christ and encourages shopping for a church where everyone shares our tastes and opinions. Those outside the church shrug their shoulders and snicker, "If they can't get along with each other, why should I bother with any of them?"

Divisions within denominations are often more bitter than those between denominations. Within my lifetime, my own church has been assailed by fractious disputes over liturgical change, women's ordination, funding procedures, and sexuality. Each of these disputes was an in-house matter, of little importance to anyone on the outside. Each consumed huge amounts of energy, diverting the church's attention from evangelism and ministering in Christ's name. Church members have attacked each other, often stooping to vicious name-calling.

Clericalism is another source of division. In most churches, clergy are given—or claim for themselves—a higher status than that afforded to lay people. One who is "only a lay person" may feel demeaned and alienated from church leadership. And since male clergy are more likely to be considered for positions of authority in the church, many women, even if ordained, feel demeaned and alienated.

Social and racial divisions in the culture at large are also manifest in the church. Most denominations can be characterized by the predominant skin color, income level, and political views of their members, as can individual congregations within each denomination. When Christians of different social backgrounds come together at regional or national gatherings, relations are usually polite, but little real learning from one another occurs.

The most bitter church divisions are usually within the local congregation, where what begins as a difference over finances, worship, or theology can become intensely personal. Those with whom one is in conflict are likely to be seated in the next pew on Sunday morning and seen at the same social event on Friday evening. Friendships and business associations, as well as congregational life, are disrupted as friends feel betrayed by one another. Clergy often serve as lightning rods, attracting anger over unwanted changes, unrealized expectations, or loss of power in the congregation. The result not only wounds the congregation, which may find itself divided into hostile opposing camps, but the clergy as well, who may experience disillusionment, burnout, and loss of self-confidence.

This collect is a prayer that all these divisions may cease and that the church may be gathered together in unity by the Holy Spirit, and show forth the power of God among all peoples.

What must occur for this to happen? H. Richard Niebuhr gave us a vision of it half a century ago in his book *The Meaning of Revelation*. The exclusively male references in this passage, which Niebuhr would surely have avoided had he been writing today, illustrate the very point he is making:

> There will be no union of Catholics and Protestants until through the common memory of Jesus Christ the former repent of the sin of Peter and the latter of the sin of Luther, until Protestants acknowledge Thomas Aquinas as one of their fathers, the Inquisition as their own sin and Ignatius Loyola as one of their own Reformers, until Catholics have canonized Luther and Calvin, done repentance for Protestant nationalism, and appropriated Schleiermacher

and Barth as their theologians. . . . We cannot understand Calvin through Fox nor Wesley through Laud. We need a larger pattern, a more inclusive hypothesis through which to understand each other's and our own memories. Such a pattern we have in the revelation of Jesus Christ. In him we see the sin of man, not of some men; in him we find the faith of man, not of Protestants or Catholics, of Lutherans or Presbyterians. He reveals the faith and the sin of all the fathers of all the churches; through him we can repent of our own fathers' sins and gratefully adopt as our own the faithful, sinful fathers of those from whom we are now separated. (p. 119–20)

We must learn to recognize the face of Christ in one another and especially in the person with whom we have the deepest differences. Catholics and Protestants must find the face of Christ in one another. Biblical literalists and liberals must do the same. Traditionalist and innovator, male and female, lay person and priest, gay and straight, pietist and activist, high churchman and low, rich and poor, developed world and developing world, black, white, red, yellow, and brown—all must find the face of Christ in the face of those from whom they feel most estranged.

To agree to differ will not be enough. To accept one another will not be enough. To reach formal agreements about historic differences will not be enough. To gather from time to time for prayer and singing will not be enough. To make friendships across lines that divide will not be enough. We must reveal ourselves to one another, gaze into one another's eyes more deeply, until we see the face of Jesus looking out at us from the depths of our opponent's soul. We must embrace the Jesus we see. Then, finally, the tears will come, of sorrow for the past, of joy for the future.

Proper 17

The Fruit of Good Works

*Lord of all power and might, the author and giver of all good
things: Graft in our hearts the love of your Name; increase in
us true religion; nourish us with all goodness; and bring forth
in us the fruit of good works.*

Beginning with the acknowledgment that God is all-powerful
and the source of all good things, this prayer offers a four-part
petition, which is an extended horticultural metaphor.

"Graft in our hearts the love of your Name." We are invited
to imagine ourselves as a fruit tree asking the gardener to graft
a branch onto it. The tree's role in the grafting is passive. The
gardener acts upon the tree, imparting to the tree a gift that enables
the tree to bear a fruit not its own. As the grafted branch grows, it
becomes part of its host tree. We are the tree; God is the gardener;
the grafted branch is the love of God's name. Left to ourselves, we
invariably choose other things, but God reorients our wills, giving
us the ability to love him above all things.

"Increase in us true religion." True religion enables God to give
its adherents the capacity to love him. False religion does not leave
room for God because it is devoted to something else: sentimentality, prejudice, tradition, liturgy, a particular view of scripture,
doctrinal orthodoxy, friendship, the desire for control or status.
Many of these things are harmless, even good in themselves, but a
religion devoted to them is a false religion. A religion that points to
God must point away from itself. Those enmeshed in false religion

do not easily come to see their religion for what it is, but there are signs of true religion: True religion does not take itself too seriously. Its pronouncements contain more question marks than periods. It does not see itself as the "right" religion, other religions as "wrong" religions. Conversation tends to be about what unites people, not about what distinguishes "true believers" from others. Laughter, joy, and confidence in the Lord are everywhere.

"Nourish us with all goodness." The tree cannot provide the nourishing it needs. The gardener nourishes the tree by providing water and fertilizer, pruning, and protecting the tree from pests. As the result of this nourishing, the tree grows and bears fruit. Since God is the "author and giver of all good things," in asking that God nourish us with all goodness, we ask for what can come only from him. Nourishing implies gradual growth. It is a process, repeated over time. Although conversion is a critical and memorable moment in the lives of many Christians, it is only the beginning. The day-to-day, week-to-week nurturing over a lifetime is what builds a Christian life. We prepare ourselves to receive this nourishing by repeated acts of penitence, self-surrender, and opening of the soul to receive the grace of God.

"Bring forth in us the fruit of good works." A tree that bears no fruit is dug up and thrown onto the refuse pile. It is not that the gardener does not love the barren tree, but that the tree does not realize its purpose and is not allowed to continue to soak up nutrients. The purpose of God's nurturing of the church is that the world be changed. Merely to enjoy the company of fellow church members is insufficient. Merely to enjoy God's presence is insufficient. Merely to believe the right things is insufficient. Our faith must be seen in holy living; our lives must manifest the devotion of our hearts.

PROPER 18

To Trust in You with All Our Hearts

Grant us, O Lord, to trust in you with all our hearts; for, as you always resist the proud who confide in their own strength, so you never forsake those who make their boast of your mercy.

When teaching the meaning of trust or faith to a group of people, I sometimes suggest we play the "blind man's game." One person is blindfolded. A second person gives verbal directions as the blindfolded person takes a walk: "Take four steps ahead. Stop. Turn 90 degrees to the left. Take three steps. Put out your right hand and feel for the bannister. Walk down the stairs. Put out your arm to feel for the door ahead of you. Turn the knob. Open the door and step outside. Walk ten steps forward. Don't trip over the big root on your left." After about ten minutes, the players switch roles. At the end of the game, they discuss their feelings of helplessness and dependency.

Some players of the "blind man's game" learn to trust their instructor and move confidently through the darkness. Others never learn to trust, resist every instruction, making every step a tentative one. Our relationship to God is based on trust. Some find it easier than others. But it comes naturally to no one. Our bent is to trust only ourselves and to boast in what we can claim as our own, as in the famous lines by William Ernest Henley: "I am the master of my fate; I am the captain of my soul." But such boasting is always based on an illusion. This is one of the major recurring

themes of the Bible. The following two citations from St. Paul
are typical:

> Not many of you were wise according to worldly standards,
> not many were powerful, not many were of noble birth; but
> God chose what is foolish in the world to shame the wise,
> God chose what is weak in the world to shame the strong,
> God chose what is low and despised in the world, even
> things that are not, to bring to nothing things that are, so
> that no human being might boast in the presence of God.
> (1 Corinthians 1:26–29)

> Far be it from me to glory except in the cross of our Lord
> Jesus Christ, by which the world has been crucified to me,
> and I to the world. (Galatians 6:14)

St. Paul mentions three things in which we often boast. Our
wisdom: we feel smugly satisfied when we can correct another's
errors, when colleagues defer to our opinions, when listeners
mark what we say. Our power: we feel a surge in our chests when
we have the strength or authority to bestow or withhold what
another needs or wants. Noble birth: we smile inwardly when
others defer to our superior social status.

Nations do the same. "America first!" shouts the proud nation-
alist. Surely every citizen of every nation wants his country to be
first, but in what do we want our nation to excel? Let us be first in
humility. Let us lead in giving and sharing our bounty. May we
excel in the compassion we show to the least of God's people and
the justice by which we order all our affairs. If we are first only in
power and wealth, then we are last in the measurements that
matter, and even our wealth and power will be taken from us. Such
is the lesson learned by dozens of mighty empires before us.

Churches do the same. Parishes grow smug. The larger ones
often become complacent as they acquire museum-like sanctuar-
ies, professional choirs, and staff members to do everything.
Smaller parishes take pride in their friendliness and intimacy,

which only those who have been there for decades experience. Charismatic parishes, Anglo-Catholic parishes, evangelical parishes, ethnic parishes, fashionable parishes, traditional parishes, parishes on the cutting edge—any excellence or gift can be turned into something to boast about. Perhaps the test comes when we tell a newcomer what we like about our congregation. Do we even mention that Christ lives there?

Players in the "blind man's game" cannot trust in themselves. They learn to trust another, or they become immobilized. So, too, Christians must trust the Lord—blindly. This does not mean we disengage our brains or assume nothing bad will happen to us, but that whatever happens, we trust God is for us, never against us. Our only boast is in his mercy. Wisdom, might, and position are ours only on loan, for God created them and, by an act of mercy, endowed us for a short time with a small measure of them. He has allowed us to "own" small bits of what he has made, but it shall return to God, to be molded and modified by someone else, when we have left the scene. We trust only the goodness of God; we boast only in his mercy.

But the mercy of God is more than letting us "own" things. God has knelt down to join himself to us in Jesus Christ. As human beings, our boast is that we are creatures to whom Christ came and for whom he died. Whether he came to other creatures in other ways, we cannot know. But if he came only to us, he came not because we deserved him more than others, but because we needed him more. His coming was an act of mercy, and it is only of his mercy that we boast.

PROPER 19

Direct and Rule

O God, because without you we are not able to please you,
mercifully grant that your Holy Spirit may in all things direct
and rule our hearts.

M any people live their lives under a cloud of guilt, sometimes
the result of an autocratic and unforgiving upbringing. They
feel unaccepted and unacceptable, and the drive to attain
acceptance is the primary motivating force in their lives.
Everything they do is in the hope of hearing deep within their
souls the words, *"You're all right. Be still, and be who you are."*

This prayer begins with a jolt that seems to confirm that
burdensome sense of guilt: without God, we are not able to please
God. All our devices to win God's favor are futile. We can do many
things by virtue of our hard work, intelligence, personality, and
piety. But none of these things will please God. We do not have
what it takes to please God. The reason has to do with who God is
and who we are. God is the Absolutely Other, the Holy One; we are
marred, broken, shabby vessels—we are *creatures.*

It was this realization that led Isaiah to exclaim in the temple
that day long ago, "Woe is me! For I am lost; for I am a man of
unclean lips, and I dwell in the midst of a people of unclean lips;
for my eyes have seen the King, the Lord of hosts!" (Isaiah 6:5).
It was this realization that led Job—known to have been blameless
and upright—to confess at the end of his ordeal, "I have uttered
what I did not understand, things too wonderful for me, which

I did not know. . . . I had heard of thee by the hearing of the ear, but now my eye sees thee; therefore I despise myself, and repent in dust and ashes" (Job 42:3, 5). Only God possesses the purity and holiness to please God.

This prayer is not, however, a hopeless one. After acknowledging our moral helplessness, the prayer continues by asking God to send his Holy Spirit to direct and rule our hearts in all things. We ask God so to fill our hearts that he will see in us his own holiness.

The two verbs, *direct* and *rule*, are both important. To direct is to point out the way. A stage director, for example, tells the actors how to say their lines and where to move on the stage. A tour director tells the tour group where to go, what to bring with them, how to behave in foreign countries. The Holy Spirit directs our hearts, telling us how to act and what to say. In directing us, the Spirit causes us to *know* what is good.

But knowing is not enough. We often know what is good even without the prompting of the Spirit, because we have reasoned it out or been taught it in childhood. But knowing what is good, we often become bogged down and do nothing. We therefore pray that the Holy Spirit may direct *and rule* our hearts. We need not merely to be directed, but to be given the power to follow the direction.

Rule is a strong word. A ruler possesses absolute power. The one ruled submits totally. We usually have profoundly ambiguous feelings about this submission: we ask to be ruled but at the same time we resist it. This ambiguity is captured in George Matheson's powerful hymn:

> Make me a captive, Lord,
> and then I shall be free;
> Force me to render up my sword,
> And I shall conqueror be.
> I sink in life's alarms
> When by myself I stand;
> Imprison me within thine arms,
> And strong shall be my hand.

My will is not my own
Till thou hast made it thine;
If I would reach a monarch's throne,
I must my crown resign;
I only stand unbent
Amid the clashing strife,
When on thy bosom I have leant
And found in thee my life.
(*The Presbyterian Hymnal*, #378 [altered])

Finally, we must not overlook the adverb *mercifully*. Something granted mercifully is a gift, neither earned nor deserved. When a jury recommends mercy, it asks for leniency to a guilty party who deserves worse. God is under no obligation to send his Holy Spirit to direct and rule our hearts. It is out of his boundless love to creatures who cannot please him that he comes, to accept, to cleanse, to forgive, and to restore.

Far from confirming or reinforcing the cloud of guilt under which many people live their lives, this prayer points the way to a brighter place, where life is lived in confidence and gratitude, in fellowship with a God who comes not to condemn sinners, but to empower them to live with his own holiness in their hearts.

PROPER 20

Not to Be Anxious

Grant us, Lord, not to be anxious about earthly things, but to love things heavenly; and even now, while we are placed among things that are passing away, to hold fast to those that shall endure.

If then you have been raised with Christ, seek the things that are above, where Christ is, seated at the right hand of God. Set your minds on things that are above, not on things that are on earth. (Colossians 3:1–2)

Anxiety about earthly things sometimes makes life seem like a journey through a barren land. Our souls feel parched; our spirits flag. Carrying with us the weight of past failures and fearing what may lie ahead, we find no joy in the present moment. As we anticipate our death, we beg to be given a serenity and peace of which we have heard only reports and rumors:

> Guide me, O thou great Jehovah,
> pilgrim through this barren land. . . .
> When I tread the verge of Jordan,
> bid my anxious fears subside;
> death of death and hell's destruction,
> land me safe on Canaan's side.
> (*Hymnal 1982*, #690)

We cannot, however, simply dispense with earthly things, nor should we do so if we could. We are, by design, earthly creatures. All that we know, we must learn from our experience of earthly things, since we have no other experience. This includes our knowledge of things heavenly. We cannot know things heavenly, much less set our minds on them or love them, except through things earthly. The things we see, touch, smell, taste, and hear on earth are God's gifts to us, signs of God's love, through which he invites us to know and love him in return.

God planned it that way from the beginning. That's what the Garden of Eden was to have been—a place where Adam and Eve would know and love God through the things God would do for them and give to them. Love of earthly things is natural and good.

We fall into sin not when we love earthly things, but when we love them only for themselves and in the wrong way. "Never was anything in this world loved too much, but many things have been loved in a false way, and all in too short a measure," as Thomas Traherne has said (*Centuries of Meditations*, II, 66).

The climax of this is the Incarnation, Word made flesh. God himself comes to us in the form of bones, hair, skin, and sweat. It is in that tangible, familiar, earthly guise that "things heavenly" are most clearly and powerfully made known to us. Because the Word became flesh and dwelt among us, we can love things heavenly and hold fast to what shall endure. Because the Word became flesh and dwelt among us, things heavenly are no longer obscure and detached from us. It is through love of the world—a world in which God has chosen to dwell—that we come to know and love God:

> How shall we love thee, holy hidden Being,
> if we love not the world which thou hast made?
> O give us brother-love for better seeing
> thy Word made flesh and in a manger laid.
> (*Hymnal 1940*, #532)

In Christ, God himself stands before us and among us, to be known, loved, and embraced, because we have ourselves been known, loved, and embraced by him.

Human life is a barren land only in our blinded perception, only if we do not see it as it really is, the theater in which heaven itself is laid bare and given to us. God has made the world and entered it in the person of his Son. The world, and human flesh specifically, is his chosen residence. We are, in fact, already landed safe on Canaan's side.

PROPER 21

The Fullness of Your Grace

O God, you declare your almighty power chiefly in showing mercy and pity: Grant us the fullness of your grace, that we, running to obtain your promises, may become partakers of your heavenly treasure.

My dearest childhood memories are those of my maternal grandmother. As a child, I often spent the night at Mimi's. I lay on her bed while she read to me stories from the Bible and Homer. A cumbersome ultraviolet lamp stood beside Mimi's bed, beneath which she warmed her bones for a half an hour each night before falling asleep. Mimi warned me that the lamp was dangerous—I was never to look directly into it—but explained that it was important that she lie under it. That was because of the arthritic joints and brittle bones that would cause her constant pain during the last two decades of her life. Mimi never actually told me that she was in pain, only that she needed to lie under the lamp. It was my mother who told me of Mimi's pain.

Mimi loved flowers and maintained three gardens around the old brick farmhouse in which she lived. I had a garden in Mimi's yard, too. Despite her pain when she bent down to the ground, Mimi knelt beside me each spring to teach me to turn the soil, sow the seeds, and press the earth around small starter plants in the little corner of her yard she had given me for my garden.

Mimi loved birds, too. Just outside her dining room window were three bird feeders. As a small child, I often ate lunch at Mimi's house. We watched the birds come to the window, as if to join us for lunch. Mimi taught me to identify dozens of birds. I learned that some birds are bold, some shy. Some are playful, some serious. Some are loners, some like to socialize.

I liked toy airplanes as a child. One Saturday morning Mimi and I were shopping at Van's 5 and 10 Cent Store. Mr. Van had six large toy airplanes hanging from the ceiling of his store. I gazed longingly at them. Mimi asked me which one I wanted. It took me a long time to decide. Finally, I made my selection, and Mimi bought it for me. The next week, we returned to Van's, and Mimi bought me a second plane. We did the same the next week, and the next, until Mimi had bought all six planes for me. Years later, Mr. Van told me Mimi had paid for all six planes the first week and instructed him to tell other customers that the planes were for display only, in order that she might have the pleasure of bringing me to his store and buying an airplane for me on six successive Saturdays.

Mimi sat for hours listening to me play the piano as a child, praising my every effort. Her favorite songs were the broad, sweeping Welsh hymn tunes of which our hymnal had two dozen or so. I learned to play them all for her.

Only once do I recall seeing Mimi cry. That was the day I released the hinges that held the ends of her dining room table together, then lay down beneath the table and pushed its ends apart with my feet, creating a chasm in the middle of the table. Mimi's favorite centerpiece had been on the table, a delicate crystal bowl that had been her grandmother's. The bowl crashed to the floor as I pushed the table ends apart, shattering into many fragments. I wanted to die when I saw her tears. She gently picked up all the pieces. Later that week she sent them off to a craftsman she had heard about who was said to repair shattered crystal. Months later the bowl reappeared, with staples and rivets holding its pieces together. It was placed again on the dining room table, but never again would it hold water.

My dearest memory of Mimi was of the time I drew a picture with my crayons on the wallpaper in her front hall. I was proud of the picture and was sure it would please her. When she entered the room and saw what I had done, she stared at the wall for a moment and then said, "Dick, that's the most beautiful picture I've ever seen!" Mimi never scraped the crayon marks off the wall and she never repapered the room. My scribblings remained on that wall until Mimi died, nearly twenty years later. Years after that, when I had married and had three children of my own, I wondered for the first time why Mimi had never removed my crayon marks from her wall. I asked my mother. "Don't you know?" my mother said. "Mimi left your scribbles on her wall because every time she saw them, they reminded her of you."

Mimi's house was across the street from the house in which I grew up. Nearly every day, sometimes several times a day, I crossed the street to see her. My mother stood on our porch as I left, and Mimi stood on her porch across the street, both watching to make sure I stopped and looked both ways. I don't recall ever walking across the street to see Mimi—I always ran. I wasn't running from anything, but to something, to a promise of unconditional acceptance that I knew would never be denied. I ran not because the promise depended upon my running, but because I wanted to leap into the arms I knew awaited me.

Mimi was a person of immense power in the early years of my life. She demanded nothing of me, yet I would have done anything for her. She never punished me, but when I erred, I asked her forgiveness. That is because Mimi declared her power chiefly in showing mercy and pity. It was a power more often held in reserve than exercised, a power manifested in giving rather than taking. Domination, though always possible, was never attempted. Mimi was always vulnerable to possible hurt by me, but when I hurt her, she never lectured or tried to hurt me in return. When I was hurt, she gathered me in her arms and applied balm as only she could apply it.

Had I used such language as a small boy, I might have spoken of "the fullness of her grace." I was certain Mimi loved me and would always love me, no matter what. It was the kind of love that would have died for the beloved. As an adult, when I think of the

love of God for his people, I think of Mimi's love for me. When I
envision God in my mind, I see a hunchbacked old woman with
gnarled hands and a wrinkled face framed in white hair with a hint
of blue. It is a beautiful face.

PROPER 22

More Ready to Hear Than We to Pray

*Almighty and everlasting God, you are always more ready to
hear than we to pray, and to give more than we either desire
or deserve: Pour upon us the abundance of your mercy,
forgiving us those things of which our conscience is afraid,
and giving us those good things for which we are not worthy
to ask, except through the merits and mediation of Jesus
Christ our Savior.*

Although this prayer does not address God as Father, the
parent-child relationship lies at its heart. Jesus was not the
first person to call God his Father, but he was the first to make
the fatherhood of God the center of his prayer and devotion.
Jesus called God his Father throughout his ministry, and the
father-son relationship formed the basis for much of his teaching,
including several parables. The term Jesus used in addressing
God, the Aramaic *abba*, is a familiar term, more like the English
daddy than the more formal *father*. In the Gospel of John, Jesus
spoke to God on terms so intimate, and his identification with
God was so complete, that his detractors looked upon his words
as a scandal. Even in the Garden of Gethsemane and from the

cross, when his agony was its greatest, he called out to God as his Father.

For many modern readers, the maleness of this language creates a problem. In Semitic culture, to have spoken of God as Mother would have seemed blasphemous. Today, however, many people find it helpful to think of feminine as well as masculine images when praying to God (the meditation in this book for last week's collect is an example). I shall use primarily masculine imagery in what follows because it is biblical and because, as a son and as the father of three sons, I find masculine imagery describes my experience. Mothers and daughters who read these words may wish to substitute feminine images in what follows.

One summer afternoon when I was nine years old, my brother Paul and I were riding our bicycles with other boys, several blocks from our house. We looked up and saw our father's car approaching. He stopped the car, got out, and walked over to us. "Come on home, boys. I've got something for you," he said. We asked what it was. He said he had bought a bat and ball and was going to teach Paul and me to play baseball. We had never played baseball and had no desire to. "But, Dad, we're riding our bikes. We don't want to play baseball," we objected. Our father insisted. Paul and I exchanged disgruntled glances and reluctantly started pedaling our bikes home.

That afternoon was the beginning of what was to become a source of life-long pleasure for Paul and me. We were awkward ball players at first: we had to choke up so far on the bat our father had given us that the small end nearly hit us in the stomach when we swung. But that summer Paul and I learned to throw and catch and hit the ball. For ten summers thereafter, we played baseball in our back yard, on the school diamond, and in vacant lots all over town. We attended the Louisville Colonels' minor league games and the Cincinnati Reds' major league games. We fell asleep at night listening to Bob Prince, Harry Carey, and Jack Brickhouse broadcasting from exotic places like Pittsburgh, St. Louis, and Chicago. By the time that summer was over, a day without baseball was a day without a purpose. Forty

years later, I was still playing ball (though when I reached fifty
and my bones told me it was time to stop sliding into second
base, I retired to the grandstand).

A loving father knows his children and provides for them, even
when the children feel no need of anything. Our father had known
what Paul and I wanted better than Paul and I had known it. We
desired nothing because we didn't know there was anything to
desire; we had asked for nothing because we didn't know there was
anything to ask for. But our father did not wait for us to desire or
ask, but gave us what he knew we would come to love. He was
"more ready to hear than we to pray," and he gave us more than we
either desired or deserved.

Our heavenly Father also does not wait for us to know what
we want or to ask for it. His gifts are often even less welcome than
those of a human father. There was nothing destructive, after all,
in my brother's and my desire to continue to ride our bicycles with
our friends that afternoon. We were merely disgruntled when told
to go home so that our father could teach us to play baseball. But
the gifts of God, "the abundance of your mercy," often require us
to abandon some destructive behavior or attitude to which we
resolutely cling and that we passionately defend. We are addicted
to evil, prisoners whose sentences have been commuted but
who remain in bondage because we do not know we are in
prison. We bring upon ourselves the very thing we fear. Our
preoccupation with self results in emptiness, ennui, death. Christ
has set us free from these things, but we will not claim the prize.

In this prayer, we ask our heavenly Father, who knows us
better than we know ourselves, to give us not what we desire or
deserve, but what he knows we need. We ask that he forgive us
those fears that keep our souls in chains. We ask that he give us
those good things that we do not know even to ask for and that
we are able to receive only because Jesus Christ has placed his
arms around us and said, *"Come with me. I have prepared the way.
I will show you the way. I will walk with you in the way. I will carry
you along the way. I am the way."*

PROPER 23

Precede and Follow

Lord, we pray that your grace may always precede and fol-
low us, that we may continually be given to all good works.

The grace of God is the goodness God pours upon us because of who God is and despite who we are. It is the nature of God to give good things to his people: God does this simply because God is God and that is what God does. It is our nature to abuse these gifts and turn away from the giver. Yet because God is God and not one of us, he continues to bestow his grace upon us. Grace precedes and follows us all our lives.

In asking that God's grace precede and follow us, we ask for what we often fail to see, and for what we fail to recognize even when we see it. That is because God's grace is often not what we really want. I recall a time several years ago when I devised a new program for the parish I then served. Others nodded their heads and said they would cooperate with me, but I had not invited them to help me plan the program, and I was the only one truly committed to it. I began to encounter passive resistance from many quarters. Then a friend asked me whether my motive in promoting the program was to serve the needs of the people of the parish or to exert my control over the parish. It was not a question I wanted to think about. My friend had seen into my heart and identified a motive behind my behavior that I could not or would not recognize. In retrospect, I see my friend's question as an act of grace, although at the time I chafed when confronted by it. I now perceive the hand of God in the confrontation, and although such things can never be proved, I feel the grace of God preceded me, moving that friend into my path at the very moment I needed to face the hard truth about myself.

Pain can be a means of grace, but we rarely recognize it as a means of grace until later. For twenty-five years I have been in a recovery program for alcoholism. As my drinking intensified and my attempts to control it became more desperate, I grew terrified of the future. My fear was undefined: I knew that continued drunkenness could result in loss of job, family, health, even of life itself, but what troubled me most was a vague, nebulous sense of terror. I saw my entire life, not merely my drinking, reeling wildly out of control. I couldn't sleep at night. I isolated myself more and more from those who loved me. Still the fear grew more intense, and I continued to drink.

Then one day I made a phone call to the right person. That friend gave me some simple advice. I followed the advice and began to discover God as more than an idea to be taught and preached about. God became someone to know, trust, and enjoy. I found a contentment and peace I had not thought possible. Looking back, I feel God preceded me during the time of my heavy drinking, protecting me from myself and leading or pushing me deeper into my fear—"'Twas grace that taught my heart to fear"—until at last I turned to him and let him put his arms around me. Had God not led me to fear, I would never have turned to him. It was grace preceding me, although I knew nothing of it at the time.

Many such experiences have taught me that God's grace does indeed precede us, even when we fail to recognize it. Philip Yancey has defined faith as believing in advance what can only be seen in retrospect. It is like being hungry and finding ourselves in the middle of an orchard. We eat, but we do not know that the orchard was planted years before by a benevolent and all-knowing farmer who saw us hungry on this day, when we had not yet even thought of the day or the place. We learn of the farmer's preparations for us only later, when we come to meet him face to face.

Grace also follows us, and we often fail to see it because we either do not learn of it or because we attribute acts of grace to mere luck or good fortune.

I have failed many times, as a parent, husband, friend, and priest. Some of my failures have been due to stupidity, but many have resulted from unbridled self-will. I have found that God follows after me to undo my mistakes, heal hurt feelings, and repair the damage I do. Sometimes I have succeeded in an endeavor only to find later that the thing to which I had devoted so much time and energy amounted to nothing—it was a mere extension of my ego, an exercise in vainglory. But God often takes these vanities and through them advances his kingdom and glorifies his name. That, I believe, is the grace of God following after me.

We see the same thing in the history of the church as a whole. Christian history brims with failure and faithlessness. We preoccupy ourselves with institutional questions and ignore the good news we are called to proclaim. We cling to power and privilege while the poor remain hungry and ill-clothed. We bicker among ourselves, occasionally even killing one another over our differences. Yet, day in and day out, on every continent of the globe, souls continue to come to Christ through this church. I can think of no greater proof of the grace of God following behind us than the healing and peace that God brings to his people by the unlikely means of the Christian church.

Does grace precede and follow us automatically? No, for if grace were automatic, our freedom would be illusory and our praying for grace an idle exercise. God does not compel us to be healed of our wounds and held in his arms. We must ask for grace, and we must be prepared to cooperate with it when it comes. Christians through the ages have found that when we surrender our lives to God, we are continually given to good works that we would never have desired or thought possible.

The great hymn said to have been written by St. Patrick while he traveled the dangerous Irish wilderness in the fifth century expresses the confidence of a Christian who trusts in the grace of God to precede and follow him:

Christ be with me, Christ within me,
Christ behind me, Christ before me,
Christ beside me, Christ to win me,
Christ to comfort me and restore me.
Christ beneath me, Christ above me,
Christ in quiet, Christ in danger,
Christ in hearts of all that love me,
Christ in mouth of friend and stranger.
(*Hymnal 1982, #370*)

PROPER 24

Glory among the Nations

*Almighty and everlasting God, in Christ you have revealed
your glory among the nations: Preserve the works of your
mercy, that your Church throughout the world may persevere
with steadfast faith in the confession of your Name.*

And the Word became flesh and dwelt among us, full of
grace and truth; we have beheld his glory, glory as of the
only Son from the Father. (John 1:14)

The glory of God is like a blazing light from the heart of God. It
fills all things and reveals to us not only who and what God is,
but who and what we are. We sometimes picture God's glory as
suggested in the Book of Revelation—a celestial scene with
heavenly beings singing the "Sanctus" and casting down their
crowns before the throne. We envision God shrouded "in light

inaccessible hid from our eyes," mysterious, fathomless, perhaps even alien. These are important images and we must not lose them, for they protect us from presuming a too familiar chumminess that reduces God to a mere helpmate or assistant to sweep the walk before us and tidy up behind us.

But it is not primarily in such scenes that God reveals his glory. The light shines most brightly not from some remote splendor, but from the face of a certain man. That man is adored not for conquests, exploits, and homage paid to him (although he could have conquered, exploited, and claimed homage), but for his humility. Born in a barn, reared in obscurity, spending his few years walking the back roads of a remote province, executed in disgrace—this is the Word made flesh, God made man, glory revealed among the nations.

This prayer links the glory of God not only to Christ but to the church, the body of Christ. The church is the primary means by which God's glory is manifest in the world today, but Christians must be careful not to take that truth for granted. The glory of God is not automatically or always found in the Christian church. When the church devotes more energy to maintaining her institutional privileges than to walking humbly in the footsteps of her Lord, more time bickering over secondary things than proclaiming primary things, the church cannot reflect the glory of God to others. The glory of God shines on; it is not within the church's power to diminish or extinguish it, but the church can exclude herself from it. At such times God does not abandon his church; it is the church that abandons God.

Despite the church's failures, however, time and again, the church manifests the glory of God among the nations. This happens in the scriptures, art, and liturgy of the church, but the glory of God is primarily manifest in the people who compose the church. A grandfather kneels to lift up in prayer the name of his grandson suffering from AIDS. A teenage boy serving at the altar winks at a girl in the choir while the rector preaches. A middle-aged woman recites from memory prayers learned in childhood. A newly divorced woman, pale and exhausted, enters the church for the first time because a friend said this was "a good place, good people." A newly married couple raise their hands in thanksgiving for the love they share. An old couple does the same. A physician volunteers at a free clinic for the poor. A mother offers to teach her second grader's Sunday school class. An alcoholic attends a meeting in the church basement. An aging soprano whose singing no longer thrills the congregation still sings "Amazing Grace" at full voice because she knows Jesus loves her. Water is poured on the head of an infant. The rector, who the day before told his wife he was unsure of his calling, stands at the altar to take, bless, and break the bread one more time. As these people and millions more throughout the world raise their voices in prayer and praise, Christ is manifest, and the glory of God, the Word made flesh, glows in his church.

The glory of God is broader than the church. We must not think too narrowly of that glory, limiting God's domain to the places and people where we expect to find him. All things shine with the glory of God, and when we pray to God to "preserve the works of your mercy," we ask his blessing on all things, seen and unseen, good and evil. As Judah learned that Assyria was an instrument in the hand of the Lord (Isaiah 10), and as Philip was led to baptize the Ethiopian eunuch (Acts 8), we must look for the glory of God in unexpected places and unlikely people. God's hand is at work everywhere about us, even in profane places and among people who speak his name only as a curse, to those with eyes to see. To "persevere with steadfast faith" is to trust God when no one else does and when we cannot see him clearly, to sing his praises when every other voice is singing a different song, to trust "that though the wrong is great and strong, God is our Father yet" (*Hymnal 1982*, #651).

PROPER 25

Faith, Hope, and Charity

Almighty and everlasting God, increase in us the gifts of faith, hope, and charity; and, that we may obtain what you promise, make us love what you command.

This lovely prayer begins by acknowledging two important facts about the Christian virtues of faith, hope, and charity (1 Corinthians 13:13): they can increase, and they are gifts.

We pray not merely for faith, hope, and charity, but for their increase. They are ours already, given to us at baptism, but they increase as we ask for more of them. Christian life is a process, more like a meal simmering in a Crock-Pot than a meal zapped in the microwave; it may be envisioned as a kind of marination in gospel juices. Christians are ever growing, ever moving from strength to strength.

Faith, hope, and charity are also gifts. They are not ours by nature and are not the result of our labor, study, or high connections. It is permissible to ask for a gift but not to insist on it. Gifts depend solely upon the generosity of the giver, and the recipient must be prepared for the gift to be denied or for some other gift to be given instead. God grants to some of his followers a liberal measure of faith, to others a liberal measure of hope or charity. He grants us what we need and what those around us need from us, not necessarily what we want or ask for. Moreover, gifts that we ask for sometimes turn out to be something other than we thought. For years I asked for the gift of faith, assuming it to be certainty of belief in religious matters. As I have grown older, God has granted me faith, but it turns out not to be a matter of certainty, but of trust. "I didn't think faith would look like *that!*" I find myself saying.

In asking that faith, hope, and charity increase in us, we are also acknowledging the fearful possibility that they can decrease in us. The events of our lives are often brutal and unjust, seemingly designed by one seeking to destroy faith, hope, and charity. I think it likely that brutality and injustice are designed by such a one— the devil is more than a picturesque way of speaking of people's tendency to do the wrong thing. Satan seeks to erode faith and replace it with meaningless confusion; he seeks to replace hope with sloth or despair; charity, with self-will. We lack the power to defend ourselves against the enemy who would corrupt and poison our souls, which is why we ask that the almighty and everlasting God defend us by increasing the gifts of faith, hope, and charity within us.

The second clause of the petition in this prayer has something of the quality of a riddle. It appears to be a cause-and-result petition: by loving what God commands (the cause), we obtain what God promises (the result). But the more I reflect on it, the more this petition seems to ask for the same thing twice. How does loving what God commands differ from obtaining what God promises? Are they not the same thing? God commands that we love him; when we love God, we experience God's love for us, which is to obtain his promises. It's a single operation that grows more and more intimate as faith increases.

According to Herbert O'Driscoll:

In our culture duty and love are often thought of as some-how being foreign to one another, so loving what we are commanded to do does not come easily to us. The great truth is that when duty and love meet, then great things happen in our lives. The Indian poet Rabindrinath [sic] Tagore has a lovely expression of this:

I slept and dreamt that life was joy.
I awoke and found that life was duty.
I acted and found that duty was joy.
(*Prayers for the Breaking of Bread*, p. 172)

Proper 26

Run without Stumbling

Almighty and merciful God, it is only by your gift that your faithful people offer you true and laudable service: Grant that we may run without stumbling to obtain your heavenly promises.

The reference in this prayer to running to obtain heavenly promises is based on one of St. Paul's favorite metaphors. He refers to running to obtain the prize (1 Corinthians 9:24), being certain not to run in vain (Galatians 2:2; Philippians 2:16), and pressing toward the goal for the prize (Philippians 3:14). But when I hear the words of this prayer, I think not of St. Paul but of my wife.

Pam tells the story of the time she attended a parade with her parents at the age of four. Tens of thousands of people lined the streets, nearly all of them several feet taller than Pam. Everyone was nudging, jostling, and pressing against one another to get a good view. In the confusion, Pam became separated from her parents. For over an hour she was lost in the crowd, confused, afraid, surrounded by tall strangers in dark coats who pressed in upon her and cut her off from the light and air. Terrified, she began sobbing. A stranger picked her up and handed her to an announcer on a high platform, who held her up for all to see, frightening her all the more. The crowd eventually parted and Pam saw her parents. She ran to them as fast as four-year-old legs could run.

Much as Pam lost touch with her parents, we lose touch with God. It is not that God abandons us—we abandon God, following the crowd into places where God is not known. These strange places allure us at first, but in time, our souls begin to thirst and suffocate. Ominous strangers surround us, and we fear that harm will come to us—perhaps we will die cut off from God. We sob with fear and grief. Then, when we had nearly abandoned hope, the crowd parts and we catch a glimpse of God again. Did God cause the crowd to part? We suspect so, but we do not stop to think about it. We run as fast as we can into his arms.

This running is characterized by unrestrained joy. It is not the fearful running *from* something, but the expectant running *to* something. Still less is it the harried, fretful running that results from fear of falling behind or being overtaken by another, leading to exhaustion and defeat. This is not a race against competitors for a limited number of prizes or spaces in the arms of God, for the prizes are unlimited and the arms broad enough to embrace a universe.

The prayer asks that we may run without stumbling. But even if we stumble, we can count on God's promise. It is not a conditional promise: "I will love you *if* you do not stumble." There is no penalty or disqualification for stumbling. We can stumble a thousand times, break our bones, and sink into the mud along the way—God will love us just the same. Nor is it a promise that can expire: "I will love you *but* you must get to me before I count to ten." God's love has no conditions and no expiration date.

The reason we want to run without stumbling is that, like four-year-old Pam when she saw her mother and father after being lost in the crowd, we see God standing before us with arms open wide, and we are eager to reach those arms. Stumbling would delay us. Eyes fixed upon God as we grow nearer and nearer, we strive to reach him at the earliest possible moment.

At the same time, we notice that God is also running toward

us. The biblical story most approximating this scene is the parable of the prodigal son in Luke 15. As the long-lost son in the story steals up the road toward his father, the father rushes into the road to greet the son. They embrace in the middle of the road, while the son is still on his journey and before he reaches his father's house. God rushes to us even as we rush to God. We may even picture God stooping to our level, as an adult stoops to a child's level as the child runs to her. In assuming human form in the person of Jesus Christ, God was "stooping" to receive us, opening his arms to embrace us.

PROPER 27

When He Comes Again

O God, whose blessed Son came into the world that he might destroy the works of the devil and make us children of God and heirs of eternal life: Grant that, having this hope, we may purify ourselves as he is pure; that, when he comes again with power and great glory, we may be made like him in his eternal and glorious kingdom.

One could divide modern Christians into two groups with regard to their belief about the Second Coming of Christ. The first group consists of radio preachers, traveling evangelists, and fellowships sometimes tagged with the demeaning label "sects." For these Christians, the Second Coming is as real as the tree in the back yard and is often anticipated in the near future. The second group includes most of the historic mainline churches. These churches mention the Second Coming in their creeds, but their day-to-day teaching and ministry rarely take account of it. One could attend a worship service every week for years in many of these churches and never hear a sermon on the Second Coming. The doctrine is discreetly passed over in theological discussions in something like the way people avoid a seedy, disreputable uncle who shows up every year at the family reunion even though other members of the family wish he'd stay away.

Why are so many Christians uncomfortable with the Second Coming? I think it is because in the past five centuries, the main-line churches of western Europe and North America have largely lost the sense of the transcendent. Sophisticated, modern people no longer take for granted the existence of a reality beyond what can be touched, measured, and managed by human ingenuity. The Bible and the church's liturgy may say otherwise, but for many people, even many Christians, God is no longer seen as moving and acting in his world. If we want something done, we go to the union hall, a psychiatrist, our congressman, a lawyer, or a doctor. Then, if all that fails, we may "take it to the Lord in prayer."

The Incarnation lies at the heart of the Christian story, and that doctrine arises out of belief in a transcendent reality. Without the transcendent, the idea that God became man, Word became flesh, is nonsense, because there is no God to become man, no Word to become flesh. Jesus becomes merely a great teacher, example, or pattern for healthy living. The reason many modern Christians are uncomfortable with the idea of the Second Coming is that their worldview doesn't allow for any comings at all. They have lost sight of any transcendent reality that might have or could have come to earth and assumed human flesh. Those who cannot see God moving and acting in his world, whose lives have not been touched, much less transformed, by the First Coming are under-standably bewildered by talk of a Second Coming.

But a First Coming there was, and a Second Coming there will be. As I read the scriptures, I note four things about the Second Coming of Christ: first, unlike at the First Coming, when the Lord came in great humility, when he comes again, he will come in glory, and no one will fail to recognize him. Second, when he returns, there will be a judgment, a separating out of the faithful from the unfaithful. Third, Christ will return at a time when he is not expected. Fourth, our job is to be ready and watchful.

The last point is the most important one. We are not to worry about when Christ will return or occupy ourselves with fancy speculations (as Christians who emphasize the Second Coming sometimes do). That would deflect our attention from where it belongs. We are to watch—but not for signs of Christ's imminent return. We are to watch ourselves, examine ourselves, make certain that when Christ comes, he will find us ready to receive him.

PROPER 28

Holy Scriptures

Blessed Lord, who caused all holy Scriptures to be written for our learning: Grant us so to hear them, read, mark, learn, and inwardly digest them, that we may embrace and ever hold fast the blessed hope of everlasting life, which you have given us in our Savior Jesus Christ.

To say that God caused all holy scriptures to be written is not to say that God wrote the Bible or that the words of the Bible were dictated by God. I'm not entirely comfortable even calling the Bible "the Word of God." We know of but one Word of God, one act in which God has expressed himself fully and definitively. Jesus Christ is *the* Word of God. When we call the Bible the Word of God, it is in a secondary and derivative sense, because Christ speaks to us through the Bible. He speaks in other ways as well, but it is through the Bible that many people first hear his voice. Christ is the only reason to pay attention to the Bible.

God caused the Bible to be written in the same way a beloved wife causes a love letter to be written by her husband. He adores her beauty, admires her character, enjoys her company, and grieves over misunderstandings and betrayals. Because of his love for her, he writes to her and about her. The holy scriptures are the writings of those who have known and loved God. As we read them, we too learn to know and love God. That is the purpose of the Bible. Some passages in the Bible (I think especially of portions of the Gospel of John) are best thought of as love songs to Jesus rather than transcripts of actual events and conversations.

This prayer suggests a progression of Bible knowledge. First, we hear the Bible. Many Christians first heard the Bible read to them as children, perhaps from a Bible storybook. This early hearing of the Word of God is profoundly important. It shapes our understanding of God and provides the foundation for the development of a mature relationship to God later in life. Adults also hear the Bible read, as part of corporate worship, but many adults, accustomed to reading for themselves, listen less attentively than children.

Next comes reading. Reading the Bible for ourselves has advantages over mere hearing. When reading, we can pause and reflect on a word or phrase. We can turn to other passages to compare. We can utilize other literature, such as devotional books and commentaries. I prefer reading the Bible in small doses and spending time with a passage, sometimes a half hour or more with a single verse or phrase, rather than plowing through large chunks of the Bible at once. Hurrying through the Bible makes it difficult to remember what I have read, while a more leisurely, reflective pace often enables me to place myself into the scene and become part of the story or dialogue.

The word *mark* is used in this collect in the sense of "Mark my word." It means to regard as important. But it is also useful to think in terms of marking in the sense of "Mark this down." Some people hesitate to mark in their Bibles. But we show Christ little respect merely by placing the book that testifies to him in an honorable place in the house and treating it like a museum piece. We honor Christ by seeking to know him, and this usually means jotting notes in the margin of our Bibles and underlining passages that speak to us. A dog-eared, well-marked Bible is the sign of a Christian seeking a deeper knowledge of Jesus Christ.

We also pray that we may learn the Bible. Fewer people memorize Bible verses today than was once the case, but learning the Bible is important in the life of a Christian, because those who learn the scriptures are never without them. Terry Waite told how his ability to recite the Psalms from memory helped sustain him during his captivity in the Middle East.

The purpose of it all, however, is inward digestion. Like the prophet Ezekiel, we must digest the word (Ezekiel 3). When food is digested, it enters the bloodstream and is carried to every cell of the body, where it not only nourishes the body but ceases to be a separate entity, literally *becoming* the body that it nourishes. We are so to assimilate the words of scripture that the Word of God, Jesus Christ, not only nourishes us but lives his own life in and through us.

PROPER 29

King of Kings and Lord of Lords

Almighty and everlasting God, whose will it is to restore all things in your well-beloved Son, the King of kings and Lord of lords: Mercifully grant that the peoples of the earth, divided and enslaved by sin, may be freed and brought together under his most gracious rule.

The year is capped with a glorious prayer affirming the goodness and power of God in all things, while also taking seriously the depth of human rebellion.

The prayer begins with a hint of sadness, like the sadness of remembering happy times long past. To say that God wills to restore all things suggests a former wholeness now broken, a former beauty now marred. We speak of restoring a monarchy, a neighborhood, a work of art, or a person's health. The word suggests the return of some good thing that has been damaged or destroyed.

What needs restoring? "All things." *All* things? We are aware of our own sinfulness and separation from God, but *all things*? The Bible speaks of principalities and powers, demons and devils, angels and archangels, as do the sacred texts of people the world over. St. Paul envisions the whole creation groaning (Romans 8:22) and St. John speaks of war not merely on earth but in heaven (Revelation 12:7). These passages hint that the brokenness we experience in our own souls reflects a brokenness in the entire creation, a tragedy of cosmic proportions. From our perspective, within time and space, we cannot be certain of the existence of other orders of beings, much less of their relationship to the Creator. Modern people, burdened by the prejudices of the Enlightenment, may dismiss such things as childish superstitions, but I expect the ancients were in touch with realities many of us cannot see because we do not look for them. Might we even imagine infinitesimal subatomic creatures on the one hand, and entire galactic clusters on the other, estranged from their Creator and panting to be set free?

We need not dwell on such speculations, for we can know nothing of these things. But such musings do point us beyond ourselves (always a healthy thing) and suggest a meaning for the phrase "King of kings and Lord of lords" far exceeding our meager experience. The important thing for us is that we, at this moment and in this place, surrender our wills to Christ.

The petition of this prayer returns the focus to earth and to the sinfulness of the human race. Two metaphors are employed. The first is the uniting of peoples now divided. It brings to my mind the crowd at a ball game. Fans are an often distracted lot. They wander the stands, browse through the scorecard, chat with their friends, shout at vendors, check scores of other games on the scoreboard, sip beer, and eat sausages. Meanwhile, balls and strikes pass by largely unnoticed. But in an instant, the crack of a bat can rivet all eyes on a single outfielder running toward the wall. Thousands of people hold their breath. A moment later, depending on what the outfielder does, they utter a collective whoop or sigh. People once divided have been united. Or recall the last time you attended a symphony and heard the musicians warm up. The sound was random and undisciplined. Then the conductor appeared and gave the downbeat, creating a unity of purpose revealed in the clear, harmonious opening chord. We pray that God will bring unity, order, and purpose to his people now divided by sin.

The second metaphor is the freeing of peoples now enslaved. To be enslaved is to be hindered from becoming what we have it in us to become. God endows his creatures with the potential to glorify him. Each creature does this in its own way. A rose blooms. The sea roars. A rabbit runs. The sun shines. A mockingbird sings. Galaxies spin. Human beings serve, worship, and enjoy their Creator—or that, at least, is our potential. But the cords of self-will bind us, and we fail to become what is in us. We pray that God will set us free from our bondage, that we may serve him as he intends. When that happens, we discover the paradox that to serve him is to be free.

Will the moment ever arrive when the will of God is perfectly realized among human beings and in the universe at large? This is a matter for hope and prayer, for we cannot yet see whether all things will be "freed and brought together under his most gracious rule." It is possible that some part of God's creation will reject his love forever. But I will venture a guess. I find it difficult to believe that anything can eternally withstand the will of God. God is stronger than all the powers, terrestrial and celestial, that rebel against him. His love runs deeper than all the hatred in the universe. His glory penetrates the darkest crevice. His wooing of his creation will continue beyond the end of time. The Son of God, who once visited a small, out-of-the-way planet, reigns over all as King of kings and Lord of lords. Nothing possesses the authority to annul the reign of Christ, and nothing can cancel what God gives to those he loves. "For I am sure that neither death, nor life, nor angels, nor principalities, nor things present, nor things to come, nor powers, nor height, nor depth, nor anything else in all creation, will be able to separate us from the love of God in Christ Jesus our Lord" (Romans 8:38–39).